The Logic of Organizations

The Logic of Organizations

Bengt Abrahamsson

SAGE Publications
International Educational and Professional Publisher
Newbury Park   London   New Delhi

For information address:

SAGE Publications, Inc.
2455 Teller Road
Newbury Park, California 91320

SAGE Publications Ltd.
6 Bonhill Street
London EC2A 4PU
United Kingdom

SAGE Publications India Pvt. Ltd.
M-32 Market
Greater Kailash I
New Delhi 110 048 India

Printed in the United States of America

Library of Congress Cataloging-in-Publication Data

Abrahamsson, Bengt, 1937-
   [Organisationsteori. English]
   The logic of organizations / Bengt Abrahamsson.
     p. cm.
   Includes bibliographical references and index.
   ISBN 0-8039-5038-1.—ISBN 0-8039-5039-X (pbk.)
     1. Management. 2. Management—Employee participation. I. Title.
   HD38.A2513 1993
   302.3'5—dc20   92-33059

93 94 95 96 10 9 8 7 6 5 4 3 2 1

Sage Production Editor: Astrid Virding

Contents

Preface

This book was published in English 15 years ago under the title *Bureau-cracy or Participation: The Logic of Organization.* The changes made to this edition are primarily aimed at reducing size by excluding a number of obsolete examples and by concentrating commentaries and critique to the classical writers in organization theory rather than to the ongoing political debate. However, a couple of fairly recent additions to the organizational literature are commented on, i.e., the research on organizational culture and symbolism—which has increased considerably in scope since 1977—and the so-called labor process literature (see Chapter 11).

The original 1977 edition also contained one chapter on participation and self-management in Yugoslavia. The recent breakup of this country into a number of independent states has led to such changes in the ownership and administration of workplaces that the earlier text is altogether out of date. The future will show whether a new discussion on this topic is merited and to what extent material for a renewed discussion can be found among work organizations in the Balkan region.

It may be tempting to make a similar argument concerning my treatment of the Marxist theory of bureaucracy. Have not the political changes in the Soviet Union and the Eastern Bloc countries shown that bureaucracy is more effectively eliminated through a movement toward the market system rather than, as Lenin claimed, through a proletarian revolution? Why, then, retain the section on Marxism and bureaucracy in this new edition?

As my discussion in Chapter 2 shows, bureaucracy is only partially caused by outer forces such as those contained in large political upheavals and changes in the economic system. To a considerable extent, bureaucratic tendencies also arise as consequences of the inner logic of the organization process; therefore, as soon as an organization is created, its mandators will have to fight tendencies among the executive to change, or even usurp, the goals and intentions for which the organization was created. Marxist theory, by being relatively insensitive to such processes, serves to highlight the necessity for taking them into account in a more complete theory of bureaucracy.

The changes in the present edition are also partly motivated by the Swedish publication in 1986 of my book *Varför finns organisationer?* now published in English by Sage as *Why Organizations?* Some of the themes that were introduced in *Bureaucracy or Participation* are taken up there and further extended, e.g., the distinction between outer forces and inner logic and between form and function in organization theory. Also, the concept of rationality, used frequently in this book but not dealt with in any detailed fashion, is given a more extensive treatment in *Why Organizations?*

For comments and criticisms of the original manuscript to this book I am greatly indebted to Torsten Björkman, Alfred Bretschneider, Annika Brickman, Edmund Dahlström, Björn Eriksson, Axel Hadenius, Horst Hart, Ulf Himmelstrand, Kaj Håkanson, Åke Sandberg, and Haluk Soydan. It is next to impossible to remember all those friends and colleagues who, during the last 15 years, have suggested changes and improvements. Perhaps this is just as well, because I am not sure that they would all find that their suggestions have been properly taken care of. However, I want to especially thank the participants in the graduate courses in organization studies at Sociologish Instituut, Amsterdam University, fall 1984; at the department of sociology, Uppsala University, fall 1985; and at the University of Växjö, fall 1988, for their interest and enthusiasm.

The library at the Swedish Center for Working Life (Arbetslivscentrum) has, as always, been the ideal partner for solving all those problems with incomplete references, hard-to-find books and articles, and recently published works that others create but librarians have to make order out of. The invaluable help from Kerstin Söderholm, Bengt Åkermalm, and Iris Frank is gratefully acknowledged.

Sandra Albrecht read the 1977 English manuscript, checked my translation, and suggested a number of highly useful changes of content and style. I am indebted to Struan Robertson for the translation of changes made to this 1993 edition.

My sincere thanks to all these people for their help and criticism. The remaining faults are all mine.

Bengt Abrahamsson
Stockholm

Foreword

In this volume, Bengt Abrahamsson, an organizational theorist affiliated with the Swedish Center for Working Life, provides an insightful analysis of the evolution of bureaucracies and the tensions between participation and efficiency that are inherent in organizations.

Abrahamsson contends that bureaucratic tendencies arise not only from factors external to an organization but also from the inner logic of the organization's processes. His presentation is clear and direct. Organizations are structures created for the deliberate purpose of achieving goals. The principal actor is the mandator — the person or collective of persons that appoints and dismisses administrator's, proclaims the organization's goals, and defines the administrator's task. From the earliest stages of organizational development the mandator confronts, often unsuccessfully, the administrator's efforts to redefine the organization's goals. Abrahamsson evaluates and integrates a wide array of theoretical works on the origin and existence of organizations and arrives at a model of organizational processes and the mandator-administrator relationship.

The author ventures into the center of an intense and longstanding debate in organizational theory and industrial sociology about the conflict between participation and efficiency, but he carefully avoids the common practice of dealing with this issue through uninformed polemics or abstract model-building. His contribution is original but firmly grounded in the classic works of organization theory; for example, he not only evaluates and integrates the propositions of Marx, Weber, and Michels regarding bureaucratization but also compares them to several American and European works on administrative theory.

The presentation is notable for its fairness and rigor; theories are appraised in an evenhanded manner and practical and conceptual problems are prominently described in the proposal for a new research agenda. At the same time, the author is not hesitant to reveal his own predilection for greater control and participation by the mandator and the subordination of the administrator. He argues that bureaucracy is not a neutral concept, organizations can function democratically, and how this occurs should be the primary concern of researchers.

Abrahamsson manages to be both an advocate and critic of the rationalistic theories of organizations and this serves him well in making a convincing case for investigating the dynamics of the mandator-administrator conflict and the accommodation of diverse interest in organizations. There are obvious applications of his approach in the study of voluntary and service organizations, ranging from hospitals to museums, as well as industrial organizations, government agencies and political parties, the traditional sites of field studies on the subject. It is also clearly relevant to my specialty—labor union government and structure. For many years researchers have grappled with the concept of union democracy and the conflicting interest of the members (the mandator) and the officers and staff (the administrator). We have written in great length about the contradictions between membership participation in union governance and decision-making on the one hand and the evolution of large, centralized union structures needed to confront employers and wield political power on the other hand. Applications of Abrahamsson's conceptual framework might help us explain why bureaucracy develops in unions and how the interests of the membership can best be reasserted.

We are presently witnessing a struggle against bureaucracy and growing pressure for democratic participation in a variety of contexts ranging from American manufacturers trying to increase productivity to Eastern European countries seeking revival after decades of political and economic stagnation. The concluding chapters of this book provide a model that is broadly applicable and true to the reality of organizational life. This revised and updated edition of the 1977 volume continues to make a noteworthy contribution to the continuing debate over participation and the emergence and consequences of bureaucracy.

Gary N. Chaison
Graduate School of Management
Clark University
Worcester, Massachusetts

Foreword to the First Edition

Bengt Abrahamsson's study is a rigorous and bold effort to present a systematic overview of the idea and reality of "bureaucracy." He reviews with clarity the classic writings on bureaucratic organization, as well as the more contemporary perspectives, and incorporates a wide body of empirical research into his analysis. His goal is a more deliberate and reasoned approach to dealing with the policy issues which he sees as required to "refute" the manifold manifestations of the "Iron Law of Oligarchy."

This study is also a noteworthy step in the continuing "struggle" to internationalize sociology. The author is a Swedish sociologist with a wide knowledge of the scholarship and research on bureaucratic organization. It is a book written in the active neutrality of the Swedish model—a critical but sympathetic search for objective understanding based on the widest possible international perspective. He is consciously dedicated to the search for areas of common agreement in the differing scholarly traditions, but is equally aware that the search for convergence does not necessarily, nor should it be expected to, produce unified reformulation.

The author is well known for his realistic research into military organization and military professionalism. His study of military institutions is no doubt one of the best preparations for this field. He is fully aware of the political assumptions and political consequences of various types of bureaucratic organization; his trenchant criticisms have pointed out that professionalism and expertise, in general and especially in the case of the military, hardly insure political neutrality.

Abrahamsson is dedicated to the central importance of the term bureaucracy for analyzing an advanced industrial society. He strives to make this a concept relevant to all sectors of society. However, the core of the analysis focuses on industrial organization, since the central issues are those of the democratic control of the work place and of the industrial sector of modern society.

His review of the existing alternative formulations of organizational theory leads to an emphasis on organizational goals and organizational leadership. He makes use of the term *mandators*—those persons who create organizations and assemble the essential resources. His perspective converges with that of sociologists and organization theorists who are interested in the linkages between the internal organizations of bureaucracies and the larger environment—that is, those who see the study of bureaucracy as an essential aspect of macrosociology.

In order both to create efficiency and to control the "Iron Law of Oligarchy," he argues in favor of greater democratization—that is, broader employee participation is required. His perspective is global. The goals of democracy are twofold: equality of influence in decision making, and equality of economic and material resources. In turn, the analysis of the merging forms of participation in the industrial sector are twofold: one is political and the other sociotechnical. The sociotechnical deals with the microlevel, the dynamics of the immediate workplace. While strategies at this level are of lesser importance than political participation, they cannot be overlooked or dismissed since they deal with real issues. At the crucial level, political participation is designed to produce basic changes in the position of the employee in the factory system. For Abrahamsson, mainly by inference, political parties and interest groups are insufficient. The internal organization of the workplace and its democratization remain the essential strategy in the long-term goals of societal change.

Abrahamsson engages in a careful examination of the empirical research dealing with the difficulties of stimulating effective worker participation in the industrial plant. The importance of the analysis rests in the fact that this sociologist, committed to an extension of worker participation, presents a realistic assessment of participatory democracy. He is explicit in his conclusion—"it carries the risk of permanenting inequalities that already exist; indeed they may be reinforced." But on balance, he sees no alternative, and he believes that the potentials for reasoned change outweigh the negative elements.

For me, his analysis indicates the clear limits on internal industrial participation in achieving the good society, and his conclusion highlights the necessity of invigorating the organized competing political parties as the final safeguard. But clearly this analysis, based on an international perspective, has sharpened and made more comprehensible the issues which social scientists, leaders, and effective citizens must face.

Morris Janowitz

Introduction

Most books on organizations are marketed as technically oriented how-to publications—handbooks on how to make changes in organizations and improve their efficiency. This kind of literature is apt to recommend itself by saying that it is empirical, nonnormative, deals with what organizations really do, describes how a "healthy" organization differs from a "sick" organization, etc. The day-to-day variations in the life of an organization are emphasized while other questions, such as those listed below, are put aside.

- In what way did the organization come into being?
- What are the conditions in which it exists?
- Under what conditions does its executive management work?
- For whom is the organization an instrument?

Much of the available literature on organizations aims to find strategies and methods to make torpid organizations more amenable to change; less hierarchical ("demolish the pyramids!"—the literal translation of the Swedish title *Moments of Truth* by Carlzon, 1985); better able to create a good climate, with a management more capable of promoting development and fulfillment; and more dynamic, more aware, less neurotic or—as has sometimes been the case—more irrational and anarchistic. This, it is thought, will create better work environments and improve efficiency.

This is a theme that is accompanied by a suspicion of rationalistic approaches, i.e., the notion that organized life may be seen foremost as planned, controlled, and predicted. Anything that suggests organization and planning is, quite simply, in bad repute in current organization theory. The conscientious administrator or civil servant is a boring person who needs to be helped toward a more flexible and daring kind of life. In serious cases he or she is referred to as a *bureaucrat,* a convenient term that suggests a combination of pest and public enemy.

The subject to be tackled is the basis on which more traditional organization theory rests in its goal-means thinking and its concept of achieving efficiency through a rational allocation of work tasks. Two names stand out as symbols of rationalist organizational theory: Max Weber and Frederick Winslow Taylor. Weber's analysis of bureaucracy is the basis of a good part of current organization theory, and much of what has been written in this field may be seen as a contribution to the discussion on bureaucracy. Scientific management—Taylor's pet interest—has had a greater impact than most other inventions on the industrial and working environment of the 1990s. Sweden is among the countries that eagerly adopted rationalization theory; since the 1920s technical advances toward more efficient production methods have had the approval of both employers and trade unions.

The growing public sectors of the industrialized nations have provided a wealth of material for the criticism of *bureaucracy.* At the same time, stepping up the already hectic pace of work in industry has directed a critical spotlight on rationalization. There has been no lack of material with which to question the classic, rationalist-based organization theories. It is natural that a large part of this literature has focused on the form of the organization and the methods by which work is governed and organized. The way work is directed and allocated, the way individual work tasks are fragmented or related to other tasks, the degree of freedom or autonomy the individual job has, and the nature of good work supervision as well as how efficiency, overall well-being, and the workplace are affected by these factors—all of these have been central issues in the organization theory of the 20th century. As I mentioned above, the definite recommendations have been largely formulated in opposition to the older theory: They cite the value of less hierarchy, less bureaucracy, less work division, looser structures, less control, and more autonomy.

What is the reason for the interest in technological knowledge in the literature on organizations? The answer is simple. The books on organizations address the need for greater efficiency and changes to the work environment that is to be found in every company and that every business executive experiences daily. Proposals for new organizational structures have an obvious target group in the executive managements of companies and government administration. There is much to indicate that companies that are capable of reorganizing are also more productive (Eliasson, 1984, p. 14). Reorganization can be profitable. It may also be profitable to publish books on how to reorganize your company.

This book attempts to draw attention to a departure from the predominant, technically oriented literature on organizations. It is my belief that this literature—perhaps precisely because of its eagerness to offer practical advice—has neglected important issues concerning the origins of organizations and the conditions their continued existence requires.

Predominant research into organizations has become so focused on solving problems—in the service of organizations—that the important questions of the origins of organizations and the conditions for their existence are often neglected. Today organizations are almost a natural part of the community and their occurrence is rarely seen as a problem worthy of investigation.

In my view, however, this very problem deserves prominence. Organizations are not a natural phenomenon: This is evident even from the simple observation that political and economic decisions can swiftly bring a new organization into existence or close down an established organization. The process by which an organization comes into being becomes of primary interest. In what way are organizations created, and what are the phases in the design of an organization, this instrument for safeguarding and promoting interests?

Words like *create* and *instrument* suggest a deliberate intention underlying the genesis of organizations. In current organizational research, rational motives have come under heavy fire. To some extent this is justified, and Chapter 7 contains an attempt to summarize the disadvantages of the rational model. But the problems to be found in the framework of rational concepts hardly justify the enormous censure it has had to withstand. Even less can these shortcomings be a pretext for accepting systems theory, the main competitor of the rationalistic model. This book takes a critical view of system-theory-oriented organization research, i.e., the research that—often on functionalistic grounds and sometimes resting on analogies from natural science—regards organizations as organisms that interact with their surroundings.

The view of organizations developed in this book may be briefly summarized as follows. Organizations are structures set up according to a plan that are designed by some person, group, or class for the deliberate and express purpose of achieving certain goals; goals that are in the interest of the mandator and that are often opposed to other interests. Organizations are used by various actors as a means for rational, planned efforts. Organizations exist to perform work, to carry out production (which may be material or nonmaterial).

However, the rational utilization of the organization as a resource is limited by certain economic, technical, and political factors in the community, factors that constitute frameworks for rational action and that delineate the areas in which the actors' motives for behavior are significant. This argument is set out in detail in Part II, Chapter 9 (particularly Figure 9.1) and will be easier to understand if the reader completes this section first.

Organizational theory has three major problem areas. The first is the question of how the organization can be made efficient. The second is how it can be made representative and how its activities can be made to satisfy the interests and realize the goals of its mandator. To improve the organization's efficiency, the mandator appoints an executive group that is entrusted with the responsibility of working for his or her goals and interests. Here, where the demands for efficiency and representativeness intersect a new problem area emerges: the problem of administrative groups that work for their own goals rather than those of their masters (often citing greater efficiency as the reason) and gradually becoming less representative of their mandator's interests. This is the problem of bureaucracy.

Since the concept of bureaucracy is in many ways of central importance to organizational theory, I have chosen to discuss it in part I of this book. The problems of efficiency are dealt with within the framework of administration theory (part II).

Formal and Informal Organization

In the field of research we are exploring here, it is frequently observed that the formal organization often—or even usually—differs from the informal organization. The organization chart, with its boxes and arrows to designate offices in the organization and the relationship between them, is an attempt by management to create structures, contexts, and guidelines for, among others, people who want a quick overview of the way their organization works.

As the critics of the rational approach vigorously maintain, it is not so easy to arrange reality into these drawing-board designs. Different kinds of informal groupings occur: Employees, who according to the diagram are not expected to have anything to do with one another, actually have a great deal of contact, whereas the people who are expected to cooperate may actually become involved in deeper conflicts. Conflicts are totally absent from rational diagrams but must reasonably be given a place in an organization theory that claims to represent reality.

The perspective examined in this book is that the frames set by the mandator for the organization's activity act as an ideal against which daily work is measured and evaluated. This ideal is often described in formal terms, comprising job descriptions, rules of responsibility, decision-making procedures, bookkeeping routines, etc. Within this structure there is an informal daily life made up of loves and hates, serious debates and pie throwing, level-headed deliberation and shows of strength. Sometimes these processes are desirable and benefit the work of the organization, but often enough they are harmful to the overall result.

What then is the "reality" of organizations? Maintaining that the informal processes constitute the real life of the organization is just as pointless as saying that the formal organization is the only meaningful subject for study. Organization theory may reasonably be expected to be capable of dealing with both of these factual areas and of adding to our understanding of the way they interact. The rationalistic starting point—with its emphasis on interests, goals, and rules—forms a good basis for this study, not least because of its direct links with legislation. Organization theory needs to encompass not only the daily events in organizations but also the frames or rationality contexts that define the actors' scope for action. To some extent these occur as political decisions codified in laws and ordinances.

Organization theory has sometimes tended to become oversociologized, that is to emphasize social—or, as it is sometimes put, "natural"—processes at the expense of framework structures. The ability to discover what actually happens in reality, rather than what is expected to happen, has perhaps been sociology's foremost sales argument, thereby casting some discredit on specific goals and purposes. To give an example, two rational actors with opposing objectives may sometimes generate results that are anything but rational. This is sometimes cited as evidence that it is impossible to apply rationalistic theory.

In the discussion below, the simple starting point is that an understanding of the frameworks for action is essential before the actual process of action is studied. Conflicts in organizations may not, for example, be interpreted in a meaningful way until we have an understanding of the field of battle on which these conflicts may be resolved.

A great many of the conflict-charged actions in the organization take place in arenas that are at a lower level than the mandator. In some degree of agreement with the employees the mandator attempts to create an organizational form that is as suited to its purpose as possible in the light of the goals to be achieved: Different degrees of hierarchy are assessed, centralization is replaced by decentralization or vice versa, matrix organizations are rejected in favor of strictly functional divisions, some administrative positions are replaced by others, etc. When experiments are carried out on organizational forms, the work climate and other factors affecting employees' well-being are sometimes given substantial consideration, and sometimes they are not. The informal organization is in itself a field for research and application and has an interdependent relationship with the formal organization. The structure of the informal organization and the ways in which it can be changed are empirical issues that can hardly be examined in a meaningful way until a study has been made of the formal organization. The occurrence of conflict or harmony is related to the conditions set by the owner and management of the organization. The degree of freedom these actors have is in its turn limited by external factors that include the economic climate, the technical conditions for producing goods and services, the statutory conditions that apply to hiring and firing, the legal frameworks for accounting and the transfer of profits, etc. Accordingly, one of the overall objectives of this book is to provide an overview of the internal and external circumstances that apply to organized activity. It goes without saying that such an investigation is largely an interdisciplinary or multidisciplinary task. Organization theory is, to an extent paralleled by very few scientific areas, a forum for broad social and behavioral scientific cooperation. An example of an application is found in Chapter 9.

PART I

THE EMERGENCE OF BUREAUCRACY
Outer Forces or Inner Logic?

1

Bureaucracy:
Some General Remarks

What Is Bureaucracy?

The concept of *bureaucracy,* in itself, condenses a development of almost two centuries of political-scientific and sociological analysis of problems of administration and government. It has been an important subject of interest to a large number of classical social theorists such as John Stuart Mill, Gaetano Mosca, Karl Marx, V. I. Lenin, Max Weber, Robert Michels, Talcott Parsons, and Joseph A. Schumpeter. The everyday, pejorative meaning of *bureaucracy* is roughly "illegitimate power." The term connotes an administration standing above and beyond the reach of the people, an administration that sometimes collaborates with power groups beyond democratic control. As I hope to show, this everyday use of the word, which is also common in daily political debate, corresponds fairly well with how the term is used by several classical sociological authors.

This political application of the term *bureaucracy* is well exemplified in an article by two Swedish trade union writers (Meidner & Hedborg, 1974). In their opinion, the expansion of the public sector in Sweden involves certain risks. The development toward larger organizational units and toward increasingly centralized administration may lead to greater bureaucratization. In such a development, the citizenry may become more and more alienated from those services, such as health care, public education, and other publicly financed activities that have been established solely for its benefit.

Many decisions which people were earlier able to check and oversee have now been transferred to regional and administrative levels less close to the citizenry

3

than before. The form of centralization which is represented by big communes, central hospitals, and standard norms for achieving economic support conveys to many people a feeling of being dominated and being kept isolated from a process in which they themselves could affect the situation, and in which they could understand why one solution is chosen rather than another. . . . There are certain dangers involved when one party—such as the Social Democratic party—is responsible for administrative operations over a long period of years. . . . The primary representatives of the party may be conceived of . . . as essentially top bureaucrats, having loyalties primarily tied to administrative strata rather than to political visions. (Meidner & Hedborg, 1974, pp. 80-83)

Interpretations of bureaucracy, and the assessments of both the social functions and political role of bureaucracy, are as numerous as there are writers on the subject. Therefore, it is quite difficult to give a reasonably clear and concise answer to the question of what bureaucracy actually is. In Nordic folklore, one encounters the mythical being *huldra,* a beautiful young woman who tempts the forest wanderer to approach her and then suddenly disappears by turning her back on him. In social science, the concept of bureaucracy has played a role similar to that of the huldra: fascinating and seductive, but evading capture in the very moment when the observer-analyst believes he or she has grasped its true character. Albrow (1970), who has written perhaps the most complete review of the term *bureaucracy* as it is used in political science and sociology gives us an impressive number of applications of the term from which to choose:

State Administration. Bureaucracy has been used for denoting the prominent position given by the centralized state power to permanently employed public officials and has been applied as an instrument of critique against this state power. This critique has generally come from liberal political scientists like Mill, who in several of his major writings opposed the concentration of knowledge and administrative experience in a particular stratum of public officeholders. Mill further pointed to the risks of bureaucratic abuse of power. "Where everything is done through the bureaucracy, nothing to which the bureaucracy is really adverse can be done at all" (Albrow, 1970, p. 22, which also has quotes from *Principles of Political Economy, On Liberty,* and *Considerations on Representative Government*). Classical Marxist treatment of bureaucracy is also related to state power. However, Marxist analysis of bureaucracy deals specifically with the administration of the bourgeois state, and thus the problem of doing away with bureaucracy is directly linked to the theory of how this state is to be eliminated.

Group of Officials. Bureaucracy can denote a group of individuals who carry out administrative tasks or an administration carried out by persons who are employed specifically for this type of job, regardless of whether it is public or private. When Weber discussed the general phenomenon of bureaucratization (not to be confused with his ideal type of bureaucracy, see "Rational Organization," below), he referred to the growth of forms of administration characterized by contract employment of officials. This kind of administration should be distinguished from administration through *collegia,* traditional leaders, notables, or groups of ordinary citizens (Albrow, 1970, pp. 40-49, 98-100).

Administrative Autocracy. Still another definition is that of an administration in which the officials exert power to implement their own interests. For example, Laski (1930), in the *Encyclopedia of the Social Sciences,* defines bureaucracy as "a system of government, the control of which is so completely in the hands of officials that their power jeopardizes the liberties of ordinary citizens" (pp. 70-74; cf. Albrow, 1970, p. 92). This definition comes close to the concept of *technocracy,* i.e., a group of technical experts who can exert power because of their special knowledge and central positions within a social institution.

Rational Organization. Here, the term *bureaucracy* is used to describe all forms of rational organization. This usage is in accordance with Weber's (1968) ideal type, i.e., it denotes a form of organization characterized by a hierarchy of offices, careful specification of office functions, recruitment on the basis of merit, promotion according to merit and achieved competence, positions salaried according to hierarchical level, and a coherent system of discipline and control (pp. 956-558).

Weber's interpretation has inspired a multitude of empirical studies, debates, and critiques. Social scientists have devoted great effort to investigating whether organizations with traits such as those specified by Weber are also optimally efficient. "It is not surprising," says Albrow (1970), "that this concept of bureaucracy . . . has appealed to management theorists since the idea of efficiency has been central to much of their writing" (p. 88). The results of theoretical as well as empirical research in this field have often shown organizations of this kind to be lacking in efficiency. For some important statements, see "Organizational Inefficiency," below.[1]

As I shall later develop in greater detail, the Weberian ideal type has served as a point of departure for important segments of administrative theory. Because of this, the concept has tended to lose its original function as an inherent element of a general and broad historical analysis concerning forms of social government. Instead, it has been employed for technological purposes, serving especially as a source of inspiration for American organizational sociology.

Organizational Inefficiency. Merton and Crozier are perhaps the two most prominent representatives of the school of thought that emphasizes "how informal and unanticipated processes, generated by ostensibly rational organization, may occasion administrative delay and public complaints of red tape" (Albrow, 1970, p. 90). Organizational means and methods marked by restraint, discipline, and routine are sometimes perceived as goals by the officeholders. This process may cause the emergence of a bureaucratic personality type (Merton, 1957). Crozier (1964), as well, uses the term *bureaucracy* to denote "an organization which cannot correct its behavior by learning from mistakes" (p. 187).

Modern Organizations. Since modern organizations often exhibit the characteristics pointed out by Weber in his ideal type formulation, it may be tempting to equate bureaucracy with organizations in general. Probably the most well known spokesman for this view is Parsons (1960), who in his *Structure and Process in Modern Societies* sees bureaucracy as roughly equivalent to "relatively large-scale organizations with specialized functions" (p. 2; for some further examples, see Albrow, 1970 pp. 100-102).

Modern Society. As Albrow (1970) points out, it is sometimes difficult to establish the borderline between an organization and society at large: "Hierarchy, rules, division of labor, careers, qualifications seem to pervade modern society, and are not simply housed in separate organizations" (p. 102). The number of organizations increases in society. If one sees organization and bureaucracy as parallel concepts (as some prefer, see "Modern Organizations," above) it is easy to view society as a bureaucracy. "The growth of organizations involves the bureaucratization of society, and that is tantamount to society becoming bureaucracy" (Albrow, 1970, p. 105). Other exponents of this line of reasoning are Presthus (1962) in *The Organizational Society* and Whyte (1956) in *The Organization Man.*

Semantic confusion is close at hand when one is confronted by such a multitude of definitions. Descriptive and normative meanings are mixed together. The concept of bureaucracy is multisided. It is used as a summary term for a category of persons with special administrative tasks, as a specific form of organization, and polemically and pejoratively as a criticism of certain trends in modern society. With these differing views in mind, one needs to ask the question What strategy may be used in order to make a reasonable pattern from this confusion of definitions?

Albrow's Solution: Reject the Term
Bureaucracy

In my view, Albrow's excellent, broad, and impressively learned book ends in an abrupt and rather defeatist manner. A major thesis of Albrow's is that the term *bureaucracy* is used, and has been used, as a label for a multitude of phenomena that have very few components in common.

In his book, he searches for a common denominator, which he feels might be found among the applications of the term made by different authors on the subject. Yet, he finishes his work by concluding that no such common denominator can be identified. Albrow (1970) does admit, however, that the concepts interlock and that they are "related, logically and historically" (p. 125), but he goes on to say that "there is no element common to them all which could form part of a useful definition" (p. 125). Although various interpretations do overlap, Albrow apparently means that they nonetheless differ enough to have few detectable similarities. Granted, they have the same name, but just as a name may denote a family relationship, *bureaucracy* only signifies that a group of phenomena are in some way related. Here, however, the similarity ends. The only common denominator that Albrow (1970) is able to find is that the term represents "the whole gamut of issues concerning the relations of individuals to abstract organizational features" (p. 125). He goes so far as to recommend that social scientists stop using the word "bureaucracy." This should not be misinterpreted, however, as a recommendation to stop studying the areas that are covered by the various definitions. One ought to "avoid the use of the term 'bureaucracy' while pursuing research in the areas in which it has been employed" (p. 125).

In Defense of the Concept of
Bureaucracy

I believe there is much to be lost by throwing the term *bureaucracy* overboard. Instead of this term, we would have to use several others, each one representing a part of the problem area covered by *bureaucracy*. But then we would not have any terms for *the problem area itself*. This problem area, as we have seen, is vaguely defined by Albrow and may be more precisely delineated. Albrow's approach is historical-descriptive. He tries to answer the question How has the term *bureaucracy* been employed in various theoretical systems and during different historical epochs? He finds, not surprisingly, that *bureaucracy* has been employed quite generously in a large variety of contexts. For this reason, Albrow seems to feel that we should be highly skeptical of the term. He seems to suggest that by lending itself so freely to widespread use, the term *bureaucracy* can hardly be of any scientific value.

There are several objections to Albrow's (1970) position. The very terminological generosity shown in his book, and exemplified in his avoidance of *evaluating* the many and diverse applications of *bureaucracy*, is what serves in the final chapter as an alibi for making a totally empty house. Instead of cleaning up among the conceptual debris, an operation that would be very natural after making such careful inventory, he simply throws it all out. This is hardly constructive, but might have been justified if it had been shown to contribute to theoretical precision and clarity.

I believe, however, that the opposite situation resulted. It is true that the term *bureaucracy* has been used to cover a multitude of organizational phenomena. But this does not imply that all such phenomena *should* be subsumed under the same label or that the use of the term in all these cases is *justifiable* or *scientifically fruitful*. The strategy of enumeration and examination used by Albrow is certainly reasonable, but it need not necessarily mean that all of the applications of the term must be *accepted*. Just as reasonably, Albrow's book might have ended with a discussion exhibiting the various uses of *bureaucracy* from the viewpoint of theoretical relevance and applicability in social science analysis. On this basis, an attempt could have been made possibly to exclude some of the conceptual variance. With the remainder, one might have been able to find common conceptual elements.

If Albrow is correct in his statement that no element common to *all* uses of *bureaucracy* can be found, it seems even more important to attempt to group together those interpretations that actually *have* something in common. Such an approach might contribute to increasing the precision of the concept instead of leaving one to disregard closer specifications as being impossible. In my view, the most reasonable recommendation is to examine in which contexts *bureaucracy* is not fruitful, and to explain why this is so. Then, what should be sought after is a definition that *if left out of* the discussion of bureaucracy would drastically reduce the meaningfulness of the term. In other words, we seek *a definition that is central and strategic to the debate on bureaucracy.*

It is my belief that the establishment of such a definition is possible. This, however, requires two operations. First, one must critically scrutinize the various definitions of *bureaucracy* (for these definitions, see discussion above) in regard to their usefulness. Second, one must make a distinction between the abstract and concrete aspects of the concept of bureaucracy. To a great extent, the conceptual confusion in the field derives from the fact that these two dimensions are not kept separate.

I shall begin with the latter issue. Often, the central problem that is dealt with in theories of bureaucracy is the contradiction between two goals. On the one hand, organizations should be effective, but on the other hand, they should be representative as well, i.e., the organizations should work for the goals of their mandators (for more on this concept, see "The Concepts of Mandator and Executive," below). Bureaucracy analyzed on this abstract level represents a *tendency within an organization's administration to disengage itself from those very interests that it is supposed to work for,* i.e., the interests of those persons who are the legitimate mandators of the administration.

Such an abstract formulation of the problems of analysis to be found in theories of bureaucracy does not in itself require a rejection of Albrow's (1970) statement that the various definitions of bureaucracy lack common elements. It is quite conceivable that the problem area might be determined in the way I have just done, but that different definitions still do not overlap terminologically. To use a metaphor, the definitions could be islands in a common sea. But even this is disputable. Looking at bureaucracy on a very concrete level, the definitions, with two exceptions to be discussed shortly, all contain some term connecting *bureaucracy* with characteristics of the administrative system in organizations, or to activities carried out by it. By *administration* is meant those organization officials who are responsible for the implementation of daily decisions, and those rules to which they are subject or that they are expected to follow.

Common to almost all conceptualizations of bureaucracy is the fact that these conceptualizations are used for the analysis of *the execution of tasks* in the service of some person or group of persons. It is the characteristics and problems of this executive stratum that are at the center of the various theories of bureaucracy and that are singled out as analytical phenomena when various writers use the term *bureaucracy* (bureaucracy encompassing here a state administration through officials, a specific group of employed officeholders, an administrative autocracy, a rational organization characterized by officials ranked hierarchically, and an inefficiency within an organization's administration). *The administrative system* is the concrete dimension of *bureaucracy* in the sense that it can be described through the use of various statistical and sociological methods of measurement. The administrative system in an organization may be surveyed through descriptions of, for example, the number of officials, their social recruitment, their education, their place in the salaried hierarchy, their formal and informal relations, task content, etc.

Essentially, the concept of bureaucracy is exhausted by these two dimensions, the abstract and the concrete. This means that if these two aspects are not included in the use of the term, it becomes almost useless for theoretical purposes. For example, if left out, it could not then be applied in the discussion of the three theories that will be dealt with in Chapter 2, i.e., the Marxist conception of bureaucracy, Weber's theory of bureaucracy, and Michels's discussion of elite formation in organizations. These three major theories would certainly fall outside a concept that is reduced in this way.

There is another compelling reason for keeping *bureaucracy* as a concept in the social sciences. If we rid ourselves of this concept, we lose an important means of communication with the intellectual, scientific, and political tradition represented in the social sciences by Mill, Marx, Weber, and many others. The contributions of these authors would appear historically and socially isolated, having no clear connection with today's problems of organizational management and organizational democracy.

Let us assume that we eliminate from our language the word *democracy*, a term equally ambiguous as the one that is the object of the present discussion. We would then need new terms for different aspects of the people's sovereignty, for questions related to direct and indirect representation, equality, freedom of communication and association, etc. The works of Plato, de Tocqueville, Rousseau, Lenin, and Myrdal, to name just a few, would soon seem outdated and in large measure unintelligible.

It is now possible to return to the first of the two previously mentioned operations needed to establish a definition of *bureaucracy,* i.e., the discussion of the usefulness of the various definition of bureaucracy with which the chapter began. Against the background of what has been sketched above, two determinations of *bureaucracy*—bureaucracy as equal to every modern organization and bureaucracy as modern society—become difficult to accept. The terms *formal organization* and *complex organization* are already coined for the phenomena discussed by Parsons (1960), and I cannot see what would be gained by applying *bureaucracy* also to the general subject of organization. For the problem of bureaucracy is only a partial aspect of the problem of organization, and in its concrete sense it applies only to a particular subgroup within the organization. It is for the same reason that one must also object to the practice of stretching the term even further to let it represent "society as a whole." As we have already seen, this determination is based on equating *organization* with *bureaucracy.* If we go this far, we are back in the misdirected terminological overgenerosity of which I have spoken above, which leads the discussion on bureaucracy back into the conceptual debris.

The Problem of Representative
Administration: The Self-Indulgent Executive

"Each form of administration," says Weber (1956), "demands some form of authority, since its government requires that some kind of power to give order is delegated to a certain person" (p. 545). When the power to give orders in the organization is transferred to the administrative system, the mandator loses the possibility of exerting direct, continuous control over the organization. The transfer of executive power may take place with or against the will of the mandator. Some dictatorial person or junta may illegitimately try to control the executive and, either by persuasion or use of force, cause the executive to rise against its masters. From the viewpoint of analysis of bureaucracy, however, it is far more interesting that the transfer of power typically takes place with the explicit consent of the mandator and, in fact, often with his or her active solicitation. In such cases, power is delegated to the administration with the goal of making the organization more effective as an instrument for the program and purposes of the mandator. As soon as power is delegated, however, the mandator may find that the administrative apparatus is no longer an obedient instrument. On the contrary, the administration may use its new freedom to choose lines of action other than the ones originally intended by the mandator. In the absence of continuous control, the administration can gradually strengthen its positions until, one day, it surfaces as the organization's ruling group and actual holder of power.

As one of many possible examples of this kind, let me use Stalin's seizure of power within the Russian Communist party during the 1920s to illustrate my case. The annual party congresses elected a central committee with wide-ranging authority to make decisions on party policy and to administer the party organization. The central committee, in its turn, elected the politburo. According to the original intentions, the latter was to only decide on especially urgent matters that might occur between the sessions of the central committee, which met every 1 to 2 weeks. Gradually, however, the work load of the central committee increased. Its members became more and more involved in the governmental tasks and increasingly had to spend their time away from Moscow. The central committee, therefore, "gradually and informally" delegated some of its decision-making authority to the politburo (Deutscher, 1959, p. 75).

Stalin acted as the general secretary of the party, and together with Zinovjev and Kamenev, was able to control the politburo. The other members were Trotsky, Tomsky, Bucharin, and Lenin. The latter, however, was ill and did not participate in the politburo meetings. No coalition able to outvote the triumvirate could therefore be formed. But for that matter, differences of opinion among the opposition generally excluded such agreements anyway. For their part, the triumvirate also dominated the central committee as well as the control commission, which functioned as the supreme disciplinary court of the party. The main conflict that eventually developed within the politburo was the one between Trotsky and the Stalin triumvirate. Stalin had the advantage of being able to control the recruitment to the party—a fact that, in the end, was decisive. Deutscher (1959) writes:

> [Stalin] used his wide powers of appointment to eliminate from important posts in the centre and in the provinces, members who might be expected to follow Trotsky; and he filled the vacancies with adherents of the triumvirate or preferably of himself. He took great care to justify the promotions and demotions on the apparent merits of each case; and he was greatly assisted by the rule, which Lenin had established, that appointments should be made with reference to the number of years a member had served the Party. This rule automatically favoured the Old Guard, especially its caucus.
>
> It was in the course of this year, the year 1923, that Stalin, making full use of this system of patronage, imperceptibly became the Party's master. The officials whom he nominated as regional or local secretaries knew that their positions and confirmation in office did not depend on the members of the organization on the spot but on the General Secretariat. Naturally they listened much more attentively to the tune called by the General Secretary than to views expressed in local Party branches. The phalanx of these secretaries now came to "substitute" itself for the Party, and even for the Old Guard of which they formed an important section. The more they grew accustomed to act uniformly under the orders of the General Secretariat, the more it was the latter which virtually substituted itself for the Party as a whole. (p. 105)

Somewhat later in his exposé Deutscher (1959) adds:

> In truth, the Bolshevik bureaucracy was already the only organized and politically active force in society and state alike. It had appropriated the political power which had slipped from the hands of the working class; and it stood above all social classes and was *politically* independent of them all. (p. 130)

There are also other ways in which the administrative machinery may become involved in conflicts over the aims and interests that it was constructed to serve. The executive may develop into a force obstructing change and innovation precisely because of its ambitions to do its duty and fulfill its obligations to the mandator. Attachment to routine and habit, to rules and paragraphs may become substituted for the long-term goals of the organization. That is to say, means become ends, discipline and order attain a value of their own, and administrative efficiency is transformed into perfectionism and overconformity (Merton, 1957). *Bureaucracy* becomes synonymous with *rigidity,* and the organization finds itself having difficulties in adjusting to changes in its environment (Crozier, 1964, chap. 7). In this way, the links with the aims and interests of the mandator are weakened, not by violent conflict but rather by slow, steady erosion.

In the debate on bureaucracy, it is hard to find any theme that outranks this one in importance: i.e., the theme concerning the contradiction between (1) the aspirations of a certain group or class to have an active and effective administration at its disposal and (2) the simultaneous requirement that this administration take maximum notice of the opinions of the masters. Thus the central object of the analysis of bureaucracy may be stated as *the problem of getting the administrators to govern the organization according to the wishes and ambitions of its mandator.* If this problem area is eliminated from the theory of bureaucracy, this theory, and indeed the very concept of bureaucracy, becomes next to meaningless. The analyses of bureaucracy try to solve the contradiction between two goals that are extremely difficult to achieve simultaneously, i.e., (1) administrative efficiency and (2) representative administration. This problem of efficiency and representation, as we shall find in Chapter 2, is a main element within the Marxist conceptualization of bureaucracy as well as in the non-Marxist social science treatment of the concept.

The Concepts of Mandator and Executive

As has already been stated, the analyses of bureaucracy typically deal with one and the same concrete object: the administrative system in the organization. By *administrative system*[2] I mean those persons who compose the executive group of the organization, the means of production that they have at their disposal and their formal and informal interrelationships that are, to a substantial degree, determined by particular rules and norms. The administrative system is attached to the organization primarily because of its relationship with the mandator, i.e., those who have established the organization as a means for achieving certain goals.[3]

I shall deal with this relationship in a more detailed fashion in later sections (see Chapter 2, "Max Weber: The Theory of Administrative Evolution," and Part II). In connection with this, I shall also discuss the question, inspired by March and Simon, of how modern administration theory approaches the problems of power and interest representation in organizations. To prepare the reader for this discussion, I shall now briefly touch on a few items of a more formal nature. First, How does one operationally define the mandator of the organization? The mandator is the party who sets up the general tasks to be carried out by the administration. Second, By what rules is the mandate transferred to the administration from its superordinates? Among other things, these rules have the function of being the basis for holding the administration responsible for the proper functioning of the organization. Thus, in this section, the emphasis is to be put on constitutional aspects. It is not uncommon for the reality of an organization to look quite different from its formal-juridical blueprint. However, it would be a mistake to ignore those formal aspects, as they are the expressions of the expectations of the mandator, and other power groups as well, vis-à-vis the administrative system.

An organization is a social unit, deliberately constructed for achieving certain goals or, more generally, for working for certain programs or lines of action. Organizations constitute resources that are means for the implementation of certain interests. Some people, usually those who have taken the initiative to establish the organization and/or have raised the funds necessary for its existence, have a more specific and usually different interest in the organization's well-being and effectiveness than do others.[4] This group of people may be labeled the *mandator* of the organization. Mandators are of different kinds, depending on which variety of organization we choose to study and partly on which theoretical interests and points of departure we may have. Mandators may be voters (mandators to representative assemblies and to the state), capital owners (mandators to the management of private enterprises), members of a political party (mandators to the party leaders), etc.

It is important to differentiate between the concept of mandator and another term that is used quite frequently by Scandinavian organizational writers, i.e., *stakeholder* (*intressent*). The translation is taken from Rhenman (1968) and will be used in the discussion to follow below. The term is used by Rhenman in a way similar to *participant* in the theory of March and Simon (1958), two authors to whom Rhenman is much indebted. The concept of stakeholder is in many ways problematical, and a caveat is called for. According to Rhenman (1968), the stakeholders of an organization may be seen to subsume a wide variety of groups and institutions. In fact, the theory does not specify any limit to the number of stakeholders. As examples, Rhenman mentions owners, creditors, suppliers, employees, the state, communes, and the organization's managing group. In Rhenman's model (to be discussed more fully in Chapter 6, "On Stakeholders") these are characterized as having roughly equal power. The firm is seen as the object of everybody's concern. Conflicts and disagreements may, of course, arise. The organization, however, strives to maintain stability. To do this, it tries as far as possible to fulfill the requirements of the different stakeholders. Through compromise, the system seeks to establish solutions that minimize conflicts (Rhenman, 1968, chap. 3).

By using the concept of mandator, I wish to stress the fact that the power relations in an organization are rarely as pluralistic and counterbalanced as implied by Rhenman. This, of course, is hardly a novel argument, as Rhenman's theory of interest balance has been subjected to fundamental criticism by, among others, Göran Therborn et al. (1966, pp. 169ff.) in *En ny vänster (A New Left)*. One may question, furthermore, whether controversies between groups that are dependent on an organization are solved primarily through compromises or whether they are settled in a more brutal manner.

Rhenman's (1968) conceptualization is made possible partly due to the fact that it ignores the historical dimension. It says nothing about the reasons why certain groups have become stakeholders in an organization and how this process is related to the organization's own previous activity. If, for example, an enterprise has a monopoly situation in the product market, customers are restricted, assuming they cannot choose to ignore the product altogether, to its offers for sale and thereby *have to* become stakeholders in the company. Yet, this is hardly a voluntary decision. The same is true when an enterprise is in a monopoly situation in regard to the supply of employment opportunities. The employees then necessarily become stakeholders unless they choose to move to another place or to stay unemployed. In both of these cases, the term *stakeholder* conceals the fact that the organization exerts power and that this exertion of power is seldom regretted by the mandator. In fact, *the explicit purpose of the mandator is often to create, via the utilization of the organizational resource, such situations of dependence.* "Thus, an increase in monopoly by a firm increases the scope and effectiveness of management authority" (Krupp, 1961, p. 177).

Since the mandator, as a rule, cannot administer the organization entirely on his or her own he or she requires a group of people who are able both to supervise production (whether material or nonmaterial) and to oversee organizational activities in such a way as to stay within the interests of the mandator. Simply stated, the mandator requires a group of people that constitutes the organization's executive group. The members of the executive are usually of two kinds. Some are elected for certain terms and are, more than others, expected to be the true interpreters of the mandator's intentions. Others are hired to carry out executive tasks. (Very often, persons in the latter category can count among their merits the fact that they have had good connections with the mandator before their employment. For example, they may have worked as supporters of a political party or as members of a trade union.) Within business enterprises, the elected members of the executive make up the management board, whereas the hired executives are in positions of managing directors and their subordinates. A parallel distinction can be made in the state organization between the concepts of government and public officials.

Who is a mandator? As already mentioned, such person or group can often be identified as the initiator of the organization and/or the partial or complete financer of its activities, e.g., through the purchase of shares, payment of membership dues, or other modes of voluntary economic support. However, the criterion of initiator is often insufficient, because an organization may and often does have a life span longer than that of the people who were its originators.[5] The economic criterion is likewise dubious, because economic enterprises, as well as voluntary interest associations, often acquire economic support from sources other than the mandator. Note the fact that the income of enterprises primarily derives from the selling of products and services, and that the financing of interest associations is often accomplished by utilizing state and communal funds.

Which definition, then, may be employed? One possibility is to start with the distinction between formal rights and actual power within the organization. That is to say, one can determine who is the mandator of an organization in terms of formal rights, leaving as an empirical question the extent to which these formal rights coincide with actual power. Almost without exception, organizations have some kind of constitution (e.g., bylaws or a charter) that states who is the mandator and how the tasks of the organization are to be defined. The mandator may, therefore, be operationally defined as the person (or collective of persons) who has the formal right to appoint and dismiss the executive group: capital owners, members, voters, etc.

One advantage of this definition is that it is fairly easy to apply in empirical research situations. Another more important advantage is that this definition does not classify everyone who is working within the organization as a member of it (cf. Chapter 8, "Who Is a 'Member'?") Rather, it views one's membership as being contingent on the degree to which a certain actor has acquired the right to take part in the appointment of the executive.

Formal rights, of course, are not the same as actual power. The intentions that a mandator may have had in setting up an organization may become eroded, transmuted, displaced, and perhaps even openly counteracted. The executive group may divert itself from the goals and purposes of the mandator, thus slowly abdicating its original function as representatives of the mandator. We shall shortly return to this problem as it constitutes the main theme in the analysis of bureaucracy and lies at the center of most of the important contributions to this debate.

On Rules and Relations

The relations within the administrative system, as well as between the administration and the rest of the organization, are determined and restricted by different kinds of formal and informal rules. I shall limit myself here to the formal rules, because the informal ones depend to a large degree on conditions specific to each organization, making a classification somewhat difficult.

There are at least four kinds of rules that regulate the daily activities of the executive. First, there are *goal formulations,* which state the general aims and purposes of the organization and indicate the recommended directions to be taken by the executive. Second, there are *procedural rules,* which indicate those routines that are to be followed in the execution of tasks and that lay down the manner in which the coordination between the various officeholders is to be accomplished. For example, there are rules for the handling and the registration of important documents, routines for employing and dismissing personnel, rules dealing with accounting procedures, etc. Third, there is a special group of rules that *delimit the area of executive competence* and define those kinds of decisions that the executive is not entitled to make. These rules, for example, may prohibit the sale of property belonging to the mandator or deal with entering into coalitions with other organizations. Fourth, there are rules that are formalizations of *requirements* directed against the organization *from external power centers,* such as state and judicial authorities. These rules usually come in the form of laws, and concern, for example, the right to classify written material, the organization's responsibilities to its employees, and the rights and duties of public officials.

Summary

Theories of bureaucracy deal with different aspects of the general problem area as sketched out above, i.e., the contradiction between administrative efficiency and representative administration. Their concrete object and unit of study is the administrative system in a particular organizational structure. This structure varies according to the interests of the analyst. To some, it is the state apparatus, while to others, it is complex organizations in general.

Different theories view the functions of bureaucracy differently, and oftentimes their evaluations of the role of the administrative system vary considerably. It is precisely this fact that makes a synthesis of the debate on bureaucracy so exceedingly difficult. That is, the *evaluations* of bureaucracy are at the center of the different theories, and it is these very evaluations that are often sharply at variance with one another.

We can now turn to the study of three theoretical systems whose evaluations of bureaucracy diverge in several important respects. We shall deal with the conceptualizations represented, first, by classical Marxism; second, by Weber; and third, by Michels. The title of Part I refers to the different explanations of the emergence of bureaucracy given by these three schools or research traditions. According to the Marxist view, bureaucracy is connected with the capitalist state and the emergence of bureaucracy is seen as contingent on the economic, social, and political changes that brought about the rise of this state. Whereas the Weberian view emphasizes the importance of economic and other power resources for the emergence of bureaucracy, at the same time it stresses the importance of various conditions directly related to mechanisms internal to the organization. Finally, Michels's theory strongly stresses an innerlogical, immanent explanation for the emergence of bureaucracy. He sees the organization itself as the carrier of forces toward increased power concentration and oligarchy. All three of these traditions, however, have in common the fact that they view burcaucratic tendencies, i.e., the transfer of administrative power to a special stratum of experts, as a definite challenge to democratic principles. They all see the problems inherent in an attempt to eliminate bureaucracy,[6] and furthermore, they see that the key to the elimination of bureaucracy is to be found in an understanding of how bureaucracy emerges.

Notes

1. A consistent theme in Albrow's treatment of Weber is Albrow's thesis that these results may not be used to criticize Weber. According to Albrow, Weber was not interested in the question of the efficiency of rational organization. "It would be quite misleading," says Albrow (1970), "to equate Weber's concept of formal rationality with the idea of efficiency" (p. 63). "The novel, unique, and for later commentators disturbing feature of Max Weber's account of bureaucracy was his utter disregard for the problems of efficiency" (p. 66).

Granted, one cannot equate formal rationality (one of Weber's main concepts) and efficiency. Nonetheless, Albrow's thesis is put too categorically. Weber himself emphasized that the bureaucratic type of administration was capable of reaching the "highest degree of efficiency" and used formulations that can hardly be interpreted otherwise than as support by Weber for the thought that bureaucracy is superior in a technical sense. As Johansson has succinctly pointed out, the German terms used by Weber to describe his theoretical creation, beautifully illustrate this. According to Weber, bureaucracy gives maximum profit in regard to *"Präzision, Schnelligkeit, Eindeutigkeit, Aktenkundigkeit, Kontinuerlichkeit, Diskrätion, Einheitlichkeit, straffe Unterordnung, Ersparnisse an Reibungen, sachlichen und persönlicken Kosten"* (Weber, 1968, p. 973).

2. The term *system* is here used only as a summary formulation for several organizational elements that should be treated together. It does not serve as a point of departure for a general system-theoretical analysis of administration. As will become clear in Part II, I am not convinced about the advantages of such an analysis. The view of organizations as "wheels within wheels within wheels" seems to me to divert one's attention from what is perhaps most central in all organizational analysis, i.e., the study of power and influence applied in a conscious and rational manner.

3. The development and shaping of these goals, like the use of organizational resources, should not be construed as a limited problem of rational choice. On the contrary, economic, political, and other factors set explicit limits on how freely goals and means may be chosen. However, subjective aspects do have to be included in organizational theory, as a partial explanation of the behavior of collective actors. "The action possibilities of each person and the number of possible action alternatives are subordinated to and encircled by external objective conditions. It is within the framework of this relatively strictly determined area that the behavior motives of the actors and their subjective orientation play a definite role" (Berntson, 1974, p. 35; see also Chapter 9).

4. More about the concept of effectiveness will be discussed in Chapter 7. However, two determinations of this concept should be pointed out immediately. According to one of these determinations, effectiveness is equal to the degree of goal implementation; according to the other, the organization is effective to the extent that the value of its output exceeds the value of its input.

5. There is cause here for stressing that the criterion "initiators" should not be confused with the initial goals that were, perhaps, important when the organization was formed. Although the original initiators may be identical to the mandators of the organization today, the original motives for the creation of the organization may differ quite a bit from the motives that are salient to the mandator today. (Regarding the difficulties of defining an organization in terms of its goals, see Silverman, 1970, p. 9; also see Chapter 7).

6. A note is justified here concerning the use of the terms *bureaucratism* and *bureaucratization*. Sometimes these terms appear as synonyms. Poulantzas (1975), for example, uses them both as representing "the political impact of bourgeois ideology on the state" (p. 332). The most common use of these two terms, however, is that *bureaucratism* is employed in a clearly pejorative sense, whereas *bureaucratization* is used descriptively to represent a growing dominance of rational-bureaucratic forms of government. In his historical survey of the use of the concept of bureaucracy, Albrow (1970) stresses the fact that *bureaucratism* has often been given the meaning "bureaucratic abuses," whereas *bureaucratization*, in reference to Weber, signifies the successive growth of bureaucratic types of organization (pp. 45-46).

2

Theories of Bureaucracy

The Emergence of Bureaucracy: Outer Forces or Inner Logic?

Some of the dominating impulses behind many different treatments and theories of bureaucracy include the conviction that it is a negative social element, that it is a repressive force and a parasite (Marx, *Kritik des Hegelschens Staatsrechts;* Lenin, *The State and Revolution*), that it is undemocratic and an outgrowth of illegitimate power concentration (Mill, *On Liberty;* Michels, 1985), that it constitutes a "new class" greedy for power (Djilas, 1957), and that it is dysfunctional and leads to the ossification of organizational forms (Crozier, 1964; Merton, 1957). Weber, too, in some contexts found reason to emphasize the risk that bureaucracy may develop into an illegitimate political force (see, e.g., 1968, vol. III, append. II).

The *normative* nature of theories of bureaucracy should be especially emphasized. Bureaucracy is described as an unnatural and undemocratic force. Therefore, it should be eliminated or its negative effects at least attenuated. But how is this to be brought about? For the analysts of bureaucracy, the answer to this question is closely related to the question of the emergence of bureaucracy. In the genesis of bureaucracy, the key to its eradication is contained. And because opinions on the causes of bureaucracy vary strongly between the different authors on the subject, it is hardly surprising that the suggestions concerning how society is going to rid itself of bureaucracy also differ, sometimes dramatically.

Heiskanen (1976) has criticized theories of bureaucracy for being underdeveloped: "The generalizations, hypotheses, and suggested theories are on so low a level of generality and so dispersed theoretically from each other that they do not have much value over and above that of sheer descriptions" (p. 115; cf. p. 108). His aim is to coordinate all formulations on bureaucracy under one common theoretical roof finally to arrive at a unified theory of bureaucracy. In his discussion, he suggests measures that are "needed in order that the theories of bureaucracy could move toward theoretical unification and proper scientific explanations" (p. 114). One such measure is trying to treat both *bureaucratization* and *debureaucratization* within "a common frame of reference" (p. 113).

This, I believe, is altogether impossible. As the following sections will serve to demonstrate, the views and ideas of different authors concerning the emergence of bureaucracy are so distant from each other as to render unification impossible. Among other things, such a unification would have to reconcile the Marxist view of bureaucracy, connected as it is with the bourgeois state, with Michels's idea that oligarchy is immanent in the organizational principle as such. Furthermore, it would have to combine optimistic perceptions of the human capacity for self-government with pessimistic conceptions that emphasize the individual's continued subordination under elites. In addition, because theories of the emergence of bureaucracy differ widely, the same is true about ideas of debureaucratization. The latter are usually contained in the former.

As we shall find, these different images of bureaucracy are also connected with different perceptions concerning the autonomy of bureaucracy, i.e., the extent to which it may be independent of its mandators. Within the Marxist tradition, bureaucracy, as a matter of definition, is seen as tied to the capitalist state, and is, therefore, a bourgeois phenomenon. Whereas in Michels's writings various administrative deformation processes tend to bring about an autonomous social category, i.e., an oligarchy, Weber is more ambiguous. He sometimes describes bureaucracy as an animated machine, activated only by specific orders. Sometimes he sees it as possessing a considerable power of its own, a power deriving from its expertise and specialized knowledge.

Marx and Lenin on Bureaucracy

Marx's conception of bureaucracy and his views concerning its social functions have to be related to his interpretation of the character of the state. The basic theses are developed in his critique of Hegel's *Grundlinien der Philosophie des Rechts* (Marx, *Kritik des Hegelschen Staatsrechts*) in which Marx attacks the Hegelian idea of the state as representative of the common interest. The contradiction between Hegel and Marx is described by Albrow (1970) in the following way:

In the great ideological systems one may distinguish two major theories of the distribution of power in society. In the one, those who held power were justified in either religious or secular metaphysical terms. They had a mission to perform for God or society and their servants, the public officials, shared in that purpose. In the other, power was the product of a group's place in the economic order of society. Officials were simply the agents of government, the instruments of the dominant class. We can see these two essentially simple standpoints elaborated by Hegel and Marx respectively. (p. 31)

According to Hegel, administration through officials is a link between, on the one hand, the state, and on the other hand, the various groups and strata in society: State bureaucracy is "the medium through which this passage from the particular to the general interest becomes possible," as Mouzelis (1967, p. 8) expresses it. Above the particular interests of corporations and local communities the supreme reason is located. It is embodied in the leadership of the state, the state executive with the monarch as the supreme head.[1] What, then, does Hegel include in the concept of executive?

In its broadest sense it includes the activities of the police and the judiciary, but since these bear more directly on the affairs of civil society they are included within it. The state executive *sensu stricto* is organized hierarchically and comprises (a) ordinary civil servants at the bottom, (b) higher advisory officials above them, and (c) supreme heads of department "who are in direct contact with the monarch." (Pelczynski, 1964, p. 126)

The public officials are the servants of the state and not servants of the king himself. Hegel's conception of the rational state includes as one important element the idea of "a corps of public servants, independent of the good will of the monarch and his Ministry, dedicated to the interest of the state and with a loyalty transcending that to any particular person" (Pelczynski, 1964, p. 102).

In contrast to this, Marx maintained that the state does not represent any "common interest" but, rather, the interests of the ruling class. The state and its executive constitute an instrument through which this elite class expresses its power. Bureaucracy fulfills the function of contributing to the consolidation of class differences and of supporting the power of the ruling class. "In bureaucracy the identity of the interests of state and of the particular private purpose is so established that the interests of state become a particular private purpose confronting other private purposes" (quoted in Albrow, 1970, p. 69). At the same time, bureaucracy has the task of concealing the actual power relationships and to function as "the general interest smoke screen between exploiters and exploited" (Mouzelis, 1967, p. 9). Bureaucracy contributes to the alienation of the people: "Bureaucracy becomes an autonomous and oppressive force which is felt by the majority of the people as a mysterious and distant entity—as something which, although regulating their lives, is beyond their control and comprehension, a sort of divinity in the face of which one feels helpless and bewildered" (Mouzelis 1967, p. 10; cf. Albrow 1970, pp. 68-70).

The Emergence of Bureaucracy

For Marx, bureaucracy is a social force through which the interests of capitalism and the bourgeoisie are implemented. The issue of the emergence of bureaucracy and of its continued existence is hence inextricably connected with the wider topic of the character of the capitalist state. Here we find the point of departure for the Marxist analysis of bureaucracy, starting with very broad formulations by Marx himself, and developed in greater detail by Lenin, and later by Poulantzas. Here we also find the reason for the continuous controversy within Marxism concerning the problem of whether the executive groups in the Soviet Union and other socialist states have become a new class or not. According to the classical view, this is not possible. According to certain "revisionist" theories, however, the existence of the new class is an empirical fact. We will return to this question later in this chapter.

According to Marx, the state is "nothing more than the form of organization which the bourgeois necessarily adopt . . . for the mutual guarantee of their property and interests" (quoted in Albrow, 1970, p. 70). In his critique of the Gotha program, Marx underscores the fact that the state can never be seen as "an independent entity that possesses its own intellectual, ethical, and libertarian bases" (quoted in Albrow, 1970, p. 70).

Perhaps the most influential further development of these thoughts is Lenin's *The State and Revolution*. In this book, Lenin comments on Marx's work *Louis Bonaparte's 18th Brumaire*. He also discusses the problem of transience from bourgeois to proletarian state and comments on the connection between the ruling class and the state's executive power.

> The centralized state power that is peculiar to bourgeois society came into being in the period of the fall of absolutism. Two institutions are most characteristic of these state machines: bureaucracy and a standing army. In their works, Marx and Engels repeatedly mention the thousand threads which connect these institutions with the bourgeoisie. The experience of every worker illustrates this connection in an extremely striking and impressive manner. . . . The bureaucracy and standing army are a 'parasite' on the body of bourgeois society—a parasite created by the inherent antagonisms which rend that society, but a parasite which "chokes all its pores" of life. (Lenin, *Selected Works* n.d.-a, p. 29)

Somewhat later in the book, Lenin explicates his thesis about the association between the bureaucracy and bourgeois interests. In a commentary to the debate between Kautsky and Pannekoek, he states that the experience of the Paris Commune of 1871 clearly shows that the state functionaries in a socialist system will relinquish their roles as "bureaucrats" or "public officials." The problem raised by Kautsky and Pannekoek concerns the bureaucratization of the workers' political and trade union organizations. Lenin recognizes that such bureaucratization affects these organizations as well, but puts the blame for this on the impact of the capitalist system. The following quotations also clearly show that Lenin perceives a basic element in bureaucracy (or bureaucratism) to be its isolation from the majority of the people.

> Under capitalism democracy is restricted, cramped, curtailed, mutilated by all the conditions of wage-slavery, the poverty and misery of the masses. This is why and the only reason why the officials of our political and industrial organizations are corrupted—or, more precisely, tend to be corrupted—by the conditions of capitalism, why they betray a tendency to become transformed into bureaucrats, i.e., into privileged persons divorced from the masses and *superior* to the masses.
> This is the *essence* of bureaucracy, and until the capitalists have been expropriated and the bourgeoisie overthrown, *even* proletarian officials will inevitably be "bureaucratized" to some extent. (p. 107)

The bureaucracy is an administrative category separated from the masses by means of particular prerogatives, playing the role of representatives for the capitalist class.

The State and Revolution, however, was completed before the big societal and political transformations in Russia after 1917. It would be interesting to study what Lenin's view of bureaucracy looked like after the end of these revolutionary events. To what degree had the attacks against the old order also meant an end to the bourgeois character of the administration and its ties with the aristocracy? Had the revolution been successful in the sense that Lenin saw as one of the most important, i.e., the broadening of the administration of society and making it a task for all citizens, thereby exterminating the "parasite" of bureaucracy?

At the Eighth Congress of the Bolshevik party in 1919, Lenin read a report on the work in progress concerning the revision of the party program. Among other things, he dealt with the problem of the so-called bourgeois experts and their relatively privileged positions. It was true, Lenin said, that the revolution had meant a substantial reduction in the salary differences between experts and workers. Before the revolution, the experts were paid roughly 20 times more than the workers; after the revolution, the relationship was something around 5 to 1. However, this still meant that the experts were overpaid and that the principle of equal pay was set aside. In spite of this, the differences could easily be explained by the need for the development of the productive forces, and this was impossible without the bourgeois experts (Lenin, n.d.-b, p. 350). Furthermore, they could not be made to work effectively if persuaded by force.

> We must not practice a policy of petty pinpricks with regard to the experts. These experts are not the servitors of the exploiters, they are active cultural workers, who in bourgeois society served the bourgeoisie, and of whom all socialists all over the world said that in a proletarian society they would serve *us*. In this transition period we must endow them with the best possible conditions of life. That will be the best policy. That will be the most economical management. (Lenin, n.d.-b, p. 351)

The need for economic and cultural rearmament was thus subordinated to the specific question of the position of the bourgeois experts. A year earlier, Lenin had admitted that this was "a step back," although a necessary one considering "the principles of proletarian power" (in the essay, "The Immediate Tasks of the Soviet Government," written in the spring of 1918; *Selected Works,* vol. VII, p. 323).

What, then, was the situation of the bureaucracy, i.e., the executive stratum that had enjoyed a highly privileged position during the tsarist regime and which Lenin had accused of being "divorced from the masses and *superior* to the masses"? Had the revolution been forced to accept an administration run by bourgeois officials? Lenin (n.d.-b), in his commentary to the party program, dealt with this question in the following way:

> The next question which . . . falls to my share is the *question of bureaucracy and of enlisting the broad masses in Soviet work.* We have been hearing complaints about bureaucracy for a long time; the complaints are undoubtedly well founded. We have done what no other state has done in the fight against bureaucracy. The apparatus which was a thoroughly bureaucratic and bourgeois apparatus of oppression, and which remains such even in the freest of bourgeois republics, we have destroyed to its very foundations. [One example is provided by the courts, which were transformed into people's tribunals.]
>
> The employees in the other spheres are more hardened bureaucrats. The task here is more difficult. We cannot live without this apparatus; every branch of government creates a demand for such an apparatus. Here we are suffering from the fact that Russia was not sufficiently developed capitalistically. [In Germany conditions were different, since the bureaucrats there were better educated.]
>
> [During the revolutionary upheavals, the bureaucrats from the Tsaristic time had been shaken up and placed in new posts. But they did not remain there. They tried to regain their old positions.] The Tsarist bureaucrats began

to enter the Soviet institutions and practice their bureaucratic methods, they began to assume the colouring of Communists and, for greater success in their careers, to procure membership cards of the Russian Communist Party. And so, having been thrown out of the door, they fly in through the window! (p. 353)

According to Lenin, the bureaucracy could be defeated only if all of the people could be mobilized to participate in the administration of the state. In bourgeois republics, this not only was practically impossible but was prevented by law. In Russia, the legal obstacles had been cleared away by the revolution, and yet the working masses did not participate in the management of the affairs of the state. Why? Lenin contends that the solution to this problem lies in an improvement of education, a rise in the cultural level of the people, and a better organization of the working class. "Bureaucracy has been defeated. The exploiters have been eliminated. But the cultural level has not been raised, and therefore the bureaucrats are occupying their old positions. They can be forced out only if the proletariat and the peasantry are organized far more widely than has hitherto been the case, and only if real measures are taken to enlist the workers in the work of government" (Lenin, n.d.-b, p. 354).

Bureaucracy had been defeated, yet the *bureaucrats* had remained in their old positions. This, in a nutshell, shows the immense practical problems that stand in the way of representative administration—problems deriving from a crippled national economy, cultural underdevelopment, and century-old, firmly established privileges. The law may be changed, the principles of popular administration may be laid down, and a certain reshuffling in the old bureaucratic stratum may be carried out. But as long as new administrators cannot be recruited from the previous underprivileged classes, the old ones will continue to "fly in through the window."

A possible interpretation of Lenin's seemingly paradoxical formulation is that the earlier function of bureaucracy (i.e., being an instrument of the bourgeois class) had ceased but that the *forms* of the bureaucratic system survived (e.g., in the practice of recruitment of personnel to the Soviet administration). According to the theory, a bureaucratic structure could no longer exist once the proletariat had established its power. Since the previous ruling class had been defeated, the necessary material and political basis of bureaucracy had vanished. The *tendencies* of bureaucratization were still a troublesome fact, however, and Lenin discussed them in several contexts (one example is discussed later in this chapter). These tendencies could be seen as depending on various "hibernating" characteristics of the individuals who formed the basis of the old bureaucracy, i.e., the information about the state that they had previously acquired, different kinds of strategic administrative knowledge, their bourgeois social background, and their generally privileged social position.

It is obvious that concession to the effect that a bureaucratic structure exists in the socialist society has far more serious consequences for classical Marxist theory than a recognition of the problem of "in-flying bureaucrats" or the existence of "petty-bourgeois elements" in the administration. The former recognition leaves the door open for accusations that state government is dominated by a new class, and that the party and state officials no longer work for the true interests of the people.[2]

Autonomy of the Bureaucracy

Following Marx's own views, the Marxist tradition treats bureaucracy as one element in the power exertion of the ruling class. Bureaucracy is perceived as organically tied to the capitalist state. This is perhaps the most fundamental component in the Marxist conception of bureaucracy. *Bureaucracy cannot be treated as an independent unit of analysis.* It must be scrutinized against the background of its direct or indirect connections with the bourgeoisie. A revolt by the bureaucracy that strikes at the root and basis of the ruling class is not possible, according to this view.

Empirically, it may appear as if, now and then, the bureaucracy gets involved in conflicts against the capitalist class. The bureaucracy is not a part of this class in the sense that it owns means of production. Contradictions between the real owners and their administrators may therefore arise. But if such conflicts develop, they can never go beyond certain limits, which are determined by "the existing forces and relations of production" (Mouzelis, 1967, p. 9). The state apparatus, including the bureaucracy, constitutes "the organized power of economically based classes" (Albrow, 1970, p. 70). To the extent that this power is undermined by economic and political events, the position of the bureaucracy will also become weakened.

As Albrow points out, it would have been fatal to Marx's theory had he acknowledged the existence of bureaucracy as an autonomous social force (or even more serious, as a particular class) with possibilities of appropriating autonomous power.

> Any suggestion that the body which merely implemented the formal arrangements of government could become a determining influence on the future of society would have run counter to the belief that nothing could prevent economic forces producing the polarization of society into bourgeois and proletariat. (Albrow, 1970, p. 70)

Here we find the reason why orthodox Marxism rejects the idea of bureaucracy as a new class. This idea has acquired perhaps its most well known spokesman in Djilas (1957), but is also represented by Rizzi (1939/1985) and by several writers within the Yugoslav anti-etatist tradition (e.g., Horvat, 1969, pp. 195ff.; Markovic, 1972; Stojanovic, 1970). The de facto utilization of the means of production by the bureaucracy and the possibilities by the party officials to dictate the principles of social development (often in contradiction to democratic principles) is used by them as their point of departure for a criticism of etatistic traits in socialist societies.

According to Markovic (1972), the dominance by the state and party apparatus has a number of fatal consequences for democracy, among others "the keeping back of initiatives at the economic microlevel, the formalization of political activities resulting in a widespread passivity among the masses, and a subordination of all areas of creativity to politics, careerism, moral dissolution, etc." (p. 126). The etatist system is dominated by a bureaucracy, which is defined as "a unified, closed working group consisting of professional politicians who control all decision-making and enjoy considerable economic and political privileges" (p. 126). The elimination of the role of professional politician, therefore, becomes an important condition for the realization of democracy. "If professional politics were to disappear as a special task area within the social distribution of work, the nature of the political organizations could be fundamentally changed. A party . . . could gradually be replaced by a plurality of flexible political organizations. . . . The significant characteristic of the political organizations would be the absence of permanent party machinery and party bureaucracy" (Markovic, 1972, p. 224).

If we, like Markovic, recognize bureaucracy as an autonomous political force, it will no longer be possible to associate it with the bourgeois state as a matter of definition. Regardless of whether one goes so far as to see bureaucracy as a new class or more generally points out its possibilities of working for its own particular interests, the making of assumptions concerning the potential autonomy of bureaucracy confronts the Marxist theory of bureaucracy with two difficult questions. First, as Albrow (1970) points out, the question of whether the thesis of a polarization of society into two antagonistic classes is tenable. Second, the question of whether socialist society can get free from accusations that a parasitic stratum has emerged, a stratum of officials that appropriates all or part of the surplus value for themselves and that acquires material and social privileges at the expense of the working class.[3]

When the revolution is still in its infancy, the thesis of an association between the bureaucracy and the capitalist state involves no serious theoretical problems. Indeed, it might well be the case that the smashing of the capitalist state brings an end to the privileges of the administrative group. Politically a polemic point may be made in showing the relationship between, on the one hand, the state power that one wants to abolish and, on the other, authorities that function repressively and generally parasitically—"standing army, police, bureaucracy, clergy, and judicature—organs wrought after the plan of a systematic and hierarchic division of labor" (Marx, 1933, p. 37).

Lenin saw that the bureaucratic apparatus did not diminish but, on the contrary, tended to consolidate itself. How did he explain these tendencies, which so clearly deviated from his theory in *The State and Revolution*? As we have seen, his solution was first and foremost to stick to the theory. The bureaucracy *had* been defeated, but the time was not yet ripe to completely transfer the administration into the hands of the people. Mouzelis (1967) comments on Lenin's "The Tax in Kind":

> Lenin explains it [i.e., the remaining bureaucracy] as a sign of the 'immaturity of socialism.' The civil war and the ensuing chaotic state of the economy partially account for it. Moreover such factors as the nonsocialist relations of production between the workers and the peasants, the still existing small bourgeoisie and the tsarist bureaucrat with his feudal mentality, constitute a fertile soil for the further strengthening of bureaucracy. (p. 12)

The key to the abolishment of bureaucratic malfunctions was to be found in the development of the productive forces.

> According to Lenin, the cure for this bureaucratization will come automatically when economic development is achieved. In the long term, it is increasing industrialization which will constitute the objective basis for a final victory over bureaucracy. (Mouzelis, 1967, p. 12)

To the extent that the means of production are socialized and production becomes more effective, the petty bourgeois strata will diminish in number and the tsarist bureaucrats will die away. Socialist relations of production will clear away bourgeois-capitalist bureaucratic remains.

Trotsky on the Autonomy of Bureaucracy

About a decade after Lenin's death, Trotsky (1936/1969) published his critical evaluation of the young Soviet state in his book *The Revolution Betrayed*. In this book, he refers to Lenin's words about the disappearance due to the revolution of the "parasite on the body of bourgeois society" (p. 41). According to the party program, the state as a bureaucratic apparatus was to begin withering away on the very first day of proletarian dictatorship. "This is what the Party program says: and it has still not been cancelled. Strange: it sounds like a voice of a ghost from out of the mausoleum. . . . Bureaucracy has not only refused to disappear, as it could have done by entrusting its role to the masses, but it has become an uncontrolled power which dominates the people" (p. 42).

But is this the same as saying that the bureaucracy has become a new class? To Trotsky's (1936/1969) mind, this would not be scientifically defensible.

> The attempt to depict the Soviet bureaucracy as a class of "state capitalists" obviously cannot withstand criticism. Bureaucracy owns neither shares not state bonds. It is recruited, replenished, and renewed as an administrative hierarchy, independently of property relationships. The individual bureaucrat cannot transfer the right to exploit the state apparatus to his heirs. *Bureaucracy enjoys its privileges in the form of power abuse.* (pp. 179-180; emphasis added)

Thus we observe how Trotsky takes great care not to fall into the trap of defining a new, third class between capital owners and the proletariat. Bureaucracy is not a class, since it does not own the means of production. The difference in actual political practice between *ownership* and the ability to *control the use* of these means may appear small. As Albrow (1970, p. 70) has pointed out, however, it is highly significant for the interpretation of, and belief in, the polarization thesis.

Although denying that bureaucracy has become a new class, Trotsky does not dispute its autonomy. On the contrary, he explicitly stresses it.

> The means of production belong to the state. But the state "belongs" to the bureaucracy, so to speak. . . . In its intermediary and regulatory function, in its concern for preserving the social rank hierarchy, and in its exploitation of the state apparatus for personal purposes, the Soviet bureaucracy resembles any other bureaucracy, especially the fascist one. But it is also widely different. Under no other regime has bureaucracy reached such a degree of autonomy from the dominating class . . . As a conscious political force, the bureaucracy has betrayed the revolution. (Trotsky, 1936/1969, pp. 179, 181)

Although formally adhering to the classical Marxist tradition by denying the autonomous class-in-itself perspective on bureaucracy, Trotsky is clear in his judgment. Bureaucracy has the character of an independent, exploitative force. Also, according to Trotsky, socialist production relations are far from sufficient for clearing away the administrative remnants of bourgeois-capitalist society.

The Elimination of Bureaucracy

The answer of classical Marxism to the question of how bureaucracy is to be eliminated has already been suggested. Since bureaucracy, as a matter of definition, is connected to the bourgeois state, a proletarian revolution against the latter will also create the conditions necessary for the elimination of bureaucracy.

The discussion of bureaucracy by Lenin is carried out within a general theoretical framework dealing with the change of the character of the state resulting from the transformation of society to communism. Kupferberg (1974) summarizes:

> After the revolution, a proletarian state is established. A proletarian class dictatorship will, during the transformation period, by the help of the state officials defend and promote the class interest of the proletariat until communism has finally become implemented. When these preconditions have been fulfilled, the class dictatorship can be abolished. However, the state will not immediately cease to exist, but rather will "die away" as the tasks of administration are distributed among all members of the society.
>
> The state will remain as an instrument to support "bourgeois law" during the transient phase which Lenin called socialism. The state will be responsible for the regulation of distribution, "to each one according to his work." But as soon as the distribution of labor has been abolished, development of the productive forces has taken place, and work is no longer a means of existence but man's most important need, the necessity of this "bourgeois law" and the last remains of the state apparatus will be eliminated. Society can, then, distribute resources "to each one according to his needs."

The struggle against bureaucracy is one of the first tasks of the revolution. In his analysis of the Paris Commune, Marx (1933) had indicated the most important steps in this struggle.

> The first decree of the Commune ... was the suppression of the standing army and the substitution for it of the armed people.
>
> The Commune was formed of the municipal councillors, chosen by universal suffrage in various wards of the town, responsible and revocable at short terms. The majority of its members were naturally working men, or acknowledged representatives of the working class. The Commune was to be a working, not a parliamentary body, executive and legislative at the same time. [The police and the officials were transformed into responsible agents of the Commune and were revocable at all times.] From the members of the Commune downwards, the public service had to be done at *workmen's wages*. The vested interests and the representation allowances of the high dignitaries of the State disappeared along with the high dignitaries themselves. Public

functions ceased to be the private property of the tools of the Central Government. (p. 40)

"This," says Lenin (n.d.-a), "is a case of 'quantity becoming transformed into quality': democracy, introduced as fully and consistently as is generally conceivable, is transformed from bourgeois democracy into proletarian democracy: from the state (i.e., a special force for the suppression of a particular class) into something which is no longer really a state" (p. 41).[4]

Thus the basic modes for replacing a state machinery that has been crushed by the revolution are (1) that each public official should be eligible for immediate recall, (2) that the salaries of public officials should not exceed the wages of ordinary workers, and (3) that administrative tasks should be simplified and allowed to rotate among all members of the commune. (Technical specialists constitute a special category. Therefore, engineers and agricultural experts are not included in the category *administration,* see Lenin, n.d.-a, p. 92.) Lenin made the following arguments.

Eligibility and Wage Equality

All officials, without exception, elected and subject to recall *at any time,* their salaries reduced to the level of "workmen's wages"—these simple and "self-evident" democratic measures, while completely uniting the interests of the workers and the majority of the peasants, at the same time serve as the bridge between capitalism and socialism. . . . "The Commune," Marx wrote, "made that catchword of bourgeois revolutions, cheap government, a reality by destroying the two greatest sources of expenditure—the standing army and state functionaries." (Lenin, n.d.-a, pp. 42-43)

Administrative Tasks Should Be Simplified and Allowed to Rotate Among All Citizens

For, in order to abolish the state, the functions of the Civil Service must be converted into the simple operations of control and accounting that can be performed by the vast majority of the population, and, ultimately, by every single individual. (Lenin, n.d.-a, p. 71; cf. Weber, 1968, p. 948)

If, indeed, *all* take part in the administration of the state, capitalism cannot retain its hold. The development of capitalism, in turn, itself creates the *prerequisites* that *enable* indeed "all" to take part in the administration of the state. Some of these prerequisites are: universal literacy, already achieved in most of the advanced capitalist countries, the "training and disciplining" of millions of workers by the huge, complex and socialized apparatus of the post-office, the railways, the big factories, large-scale commerce, banking, etc. etc. . . . . *All* citizens become employees and workers of a *single,* national state syndicate. All that is required is that they should work equally—do their proper share of work—and get paid equally. The accounting and control necessary for this have been so utterly *simplified* by capitalism that they have become the extraordinarily simple operations of checking, recording and issuing receipts, which anyone who can read or write and who knows the first four rules of arithmetic can perform. (Lenin, n.d.-a, pp. 92-93)

In communist society, where no exploitation and no class differences exist, bureaucracy becomes superfluous. Bureaucracy is "absorbed" by society (Mouzelis, 1967, p. 11), and the administrative tasks lose their exploitive character. In the new society, the administrative system occupies itself with the administration of things and not, as was the case with bourgeois bureaucracy, the administration of people. The development of the productive forces creates, first, the possibilities of education for all, and second, the preconditions for the simplification of administrative operations so that an elementary knowledge of writing and arithmetic is sufficient for mastering them. It is in this way, according to Lenin, that it becomes possible to distribute administrative tasks among all citizens (with the exception of the technical specialists whose services society could not do without), and as a consequence, to give everyone equal remuneration for his services.

I will not discuss in this context the reasonableness of the preconditions on which Lenin bases his program for the elimination of bureaucracy, nor will I comment on the observable deviations of Soviet society from Lenin's model. However, I do want to stress that the solutions to the problems of bureaucracy must be one of the most important undertakings in any attempt to realize a system capable of self-government. The problems brought up by Lenin, and which were based on Marx's analysis of the Paris Commune, reappears with full force among proponents of the syndicalist movement (see, e.g., Håkanson, 1973) and also among several social scientists who have been occupied with criticizing and suggesting changes in the Yugoslav associationist-socialist system (see, e.g., Horvat, 1969, chaps. 3-5; Markovic, 1972, esp. chaps. 5, 7, 11). The questions that they have tried to answer, among others, are

1. Does the development of the productive forces really imply that the administrative tasks are simplified?[5]
2. Is it possible to obtain optimum efficiency in a system of equal pay?[6]
3. How is one to avoid the drawbacks inherent in the rotation of tasks, i.e., the lack of continuity in work and the loss of the valuable experience that the administrators would get through the very process of working?[7]

4. Will the technical specialists, who probably could not be incorporated into the equal pay system but who rather would have to be stimulated through the use of economic incentives, get an unacceptably privileged position in society?

5. How is one to avoid the professionalization of administrative and political positions? That is, how does one avoid the risk that these officials will acquire the same advantages as the technical specialists?

Thus, briefly, the problems that confront Lenin's model of debureaucratization are dependent to a great degree on what Lenin saw as the long-run solution for the elimination of bureaucracy, i.e., the intensification of the productive forces. On the one hand, we find that a precondition for this intensification would be the proper cultivation of technical, scientific, and administrative competence. But on the other hand, we see that to make this cultivation as effective as possible, at least a certain amount of distribution of work tasks would become necessary. This, of course, involves risks of professionalization, permanence in positions, economic advantages and other social privileges. Furthermore, officials may attempt to consolidate their own positions by making their tasks appear too complicated to be executed by others (cf. Germain, 1969, pp. 4ff.).

Max Weber: The Theory of Administrative Evolution

Weber perceived the capitalist order of production as *one* important driving force for the emergence of bureaucratic patterns of organization. According to him, bureaucracy was a product of a general development of society toward rational, goal-oriented organized behavior. In this development, capitalism played a major role. In contrast to Marx and Lenin, Weber did not see bureaucracy as a specific bourgeois phenomenon tied to capitalism and thus destined to vanish with the disappearance of capitalism. Rather, bureaucracy was seen as an independent entity, surviving in society, be it capitalist or socialist.

In his treatment of the emergence of bureaucracy, Weber worked with a multifactor model wherein economic variables constituted the most crucial elements. Since the rise of bureaucracy is conditioned by those factors that have created the "modern" society, i.e., capitalism, centralization tendencies, and "mass democracy," it is a phenomenon that cannot be eliminated. It is an indispensable component of a society built on a complex distribution of labor, centralized administration, and money economy. It simply cannot be done away with. "If bureaucratic administration is, other things being equal, always the most rational type from a technical point of view, the needs of mass administration make it today completely indispensable. The choice is only that between bureaucracy and dilettantism in the field of administration" (Weber, 1968, p. 223).[8]

Bureaucracy has become a permanent social force. Its superiority derives from its character of being an impersonal apparatus, technically competent, precise and disciplined. But could this apparatus, exactly because of its competence, become the master of its masters, overthrowing its mandators? Where did Weber actually stand on this issue of the possible autonomy of bureaucracy and its ability to act on its own behalf? What did he say on the issue of bureaucratic autonomy, which Marxism denies as a matter of definition? As we shall see, it is difficult to find in Weber's writings any definite opinion on this point. In certain contexts he strongly stressed the subordination of bureaucracy (*straffe Unterordnung*) and its capability of being an obedient instrument to any holder of power. In other contexts, however, he saw it as a sovereign power in itself with own vested interests for the preservation of the social system.

Weber on the Emergence of Bureaucracy

According to Weber,[9] there are several historical examples of bureaucratic forms of administration. One such example is that of Egypt during the period of the New Kingdom where the need for centralized control of water regulations and the construction of an irrigation system demanded a vast staff of officials. Other examples can be found in the later Roman Principate, in China during the time of Shi Hwangti and up to 1900, and in the Roman Catholic church, particularly after the 13th century (Weber, 1968, pp. 964, 972). However, the bureaucratic systems in these cases had certain feudal nepotistic characteristics and were also partially based on remuneration in natura to the officials. They are not, therefore, pure examples of bureaucracies.

Bureaucracy, in the form we know it today, appeared in the European states in increasingly pure form concurrently with the growth of the absolute kingdoms. An important precondition for the spread and consolidation of bureaucracy was the creation of a *money economy,* the rules of which became more strongly emphasized when the European states began to develop in a capitalist direction. "The large modern capitalist enterprise" is perhaps Weber's (1968, p. 964) foremost example of the application of bureaucratic principles of administration.

The development of the *money economy* is a presupposition of a modern bureaucracy insofar as the compensation of officials today takes the form of money salaries. The money economy is of very great importance for the whole bearing of bureaucracy, yet by itself it is by no means decisive for the existence of bureaucracy. . . . [At this point there follow the examples of early bureaucracies which were mentioned above.] A certain measure of a developed money economy is the normal precondition at least for the unchanged survival, if not for the establishment, of pure bureaucratic administrations. (Weber, 1968, pp. 963-964)

A distinctive trait of Weber is his reluctance to designate a particular factor as *the most important* or *key factor* in a causal sense.[10] Even in his explanation of the emergence of bureaucracy, he is, as was shown in the quotation above, anxious to avoid emphasizing the money economy as the most important cause, even though it is obvious that few factors outrank it in importance. It may be that a money economy is not an "indispensable precondition" for bureaucratization, says Weber. Yet bureaucracy as a permanent structure is "knit to the one presupposition of the availability of continuous revenues to maintain it." When such income cannot be taken from private profits (as in modern enterprises, for example) or from land rents (as in the case of big estates), then a permanent *taxation system* is necessary in order for a system of bureaucratic administration to prevail. And, "for well-known general reasons, only a fully developed money economy offers a secure basis for such a taxation system" (Weber, 1968, p. 968). A society where remuneration to the working people is given in the form of money, and where the tasks and undertakings of the state have to be financed through taxation, requires a staff of administrative officials that can exercise a degree of control while performing bookkeeping and money-collecting activities.

It is not only within private capitalist enterprises and modern state administrations that Weber observes tendencies of bureaucratization. He also stresses how the modern army, the church, and the universities have gradually lost their traditional archaic characteristics. He finds that they are increasingly administered by impersonal and rational rules aimed at attaining maximum efficiency. Weber's exposition is a methodical review of factors that generally work in the direction of bureaucratization, an inventory filled with numerous examples of how organizations become bureaucratized. In addition to a money economy, on which I have already commented, the following factors as well are part of Weber's sketch.

Standing Armies. Power motives and expansionist strivings of national states produce a necessity for permanent military forces. Since money has to be collected to finance the armies and the war enterprises, a corps of

Max Weber—Legal Authority: The Pure Type

The purest type of exercise of legal authority is that which employs a bureaucratic administrative staff. Only the supreme chief of the organization occupies his or her position of dominance (*Herrenstellung*) by virtue of appropriation, of election, or of having been designated for the succession. But even *his or her* authority consists in a sphere of legal competence. The whole administrative staff under the supreme authority then consists, in the purest type, of individual officials . . . who are appointed and function according to the following criteria:

1. They are personally free and subject to authority only with respect to their impersonal official obligations.
2. They are organized in a clearly defined hierarchy of offices.
3. Each office has a clearly defined sphere of competence in the legal sense.
4. The office is filled by a free contractual relationship. Thus, in principle, there is free selection.
5. Candidates are selected on the basis of technical qualifications. In the most rational case, this is tested by examinations or guaranteed by diplomas certifying technical training, or both. They are *appointed,* not elected.
6. They are remunerated by fixed salaries in money, for the most part with the right to pension. The salary scale is graded according to rank in the hierarchy, but in addition to this criterion, the responsibility of the position and the requirements of the incumbent's social status may be taken into account.
7. The office is treated as the sole, or at least the primary, occupation of the incumbent.
8. It constitutes a career. There is a system of promotion, according to seniority or to achievement or to both. Promotion is dependent on the judgment of superiors.
9. The official works entirely separated from ownership of the means of administration and without appropriation of his position.
10. He or she is subject to strict and systematic discipline and control in the conduct of the office.

SOURCE: Weber (1968, pp. 220-221)

functionaries comes into existence for this purpose. Weber also posits the idea that armies tend to become more and more organizationally differentiated, in and of themselves, and subsequently, more bureaucratized.

Material Wealth. Greater material affluence and a raised standard of living are accompanied by the need for the public sector to play an increasingly active role in the management of the state. A growing number of social services begin to be seen as indispensable, with the result being that bureaucratic forms of management are employed to fulfill needs that previously were performed either locally or through the private sector (Weber, 1968, p. 972).

Modern Means of Communication. The administration of modern Western society is possible only if the state takes control of telegraph communications, mail distribution, and the railroads (Weber, 1968, p. 973).

Political Factors. Universal suffrage and the rise of the institution of mass political parties, both of which are associated with general voting rights, are factors of utmost importance for the spread of bureaucracy. Here, Weber is close to being categorical and far less restrictive than in his previous causal explanations.

> Bureaucracy inevitably accompanies modern *mass democracy,* in contrast to the democratic self-government of small homogeneous units. . . . Mass democracy, which makes a clean sweep of the feudal, patrimonial, and—at least in intent—the plutocratic privileges in administration unavoidably has to put paid professional labor in place of the historically inherited "avocational" administration by notables [as e.g., the landlords of eastern Prussia]. (Weber, 1968, pp. 983-984)

In his reflections on the need of the modern party institutions for professional administrators, Weber strongly resembles Michels (see "The Emergence of Elite Rule," below). Michels, however, ties his analysis of the bureaucratic tendencies in party organizations to strong deterministic presuppositions concerning the inevitability of the concentration of power into an oligarchy. Although Weber was far from silent about the power abuse and antidemocratic aspects of bureaucratization, he was nonetheless cautious about implying that bureaucratized politics must *necessarily* lead to a reordering of the administration in the direction of oligarchy. Nevertheless, it is obvious that Weber was aware that the *size* of political organization in itself is a force toward increased bureaucratization. Both direct democracy and government by notables are "technically inade-

quate" in "organizations beyond a certain limit of size, constituting more
than a few thousand full-fledged members" (Weber, 1968, p. 291). The
participation of every individual in the governing of an organization is
possible only in small associations of an egalitarian nature. In such associations, direct democracy can be implemented via various technical
arrangements, for example, by rotating officials, by having short mandate
periods, and by using the notion of recallability (Weber, 1968, pp. 289,
948; cf. Lenin's blueprint for debureaucratization in *The State and Revolution,* discussed earlier in this chapter). However, the larger the organization becomes, the greater is the difficulty in sustaining these principles.
According to Weber (1968), excellent examples of this relationship between an organization's size and its tendency toward bureaucratization can
be found in the case of the German Social Democratic party, and the U.S.
Democratic and Republican parties (p. 971).

In his writings on the importance of the size factor, Weber comes close
to the innerlogical explanations of the emergence of oligarchy espoused
by Michels (1958) in his book *Political Parties.* Weber's writings, in
contrast to Michels's, stress the idea that immanent factors only represent
one element in the explanation of the rise of bureaucracy. To Weber, the
macrorelationships involving economic, political, and technological
transformations were equally as important for the emergence and existence of bureaucratic forms of administration as were immanent factors.
Weber's concept of bureaucracy cannot be properly understood unless
seen within the erudite, historically insightful, and broadly displayed
sociological and political-scientific framework that he provided. Unfortu-
nately, this framework has all too often been ignored by organizational
sociologists. A few words about this are in order.

Bureaucracy, Capitalism, and Organizational Sociology

As has often been pointed out (e.g., Sunesson, 1974, pp. 59-68), the
sociology of organizations that has arisen and developed during the 20th
century has largely consisted of commentaries to, and modifications of,
Weber's ideal-typical concept of bureaucracy. One school of thought
within organizational sociology has questioned whether bureaucracy is
actually as rational as Weber claimed (Crozier, 1964; Merton, 1957). Other
social scientists, partly inspired by Weber, have tried to develop various
typologies of organizations (e.g., Blau & Scott, 1962; Burns & Stalker,
1961; Etzioni, 1964). Still others have focused on the individual and his
or her adjustment to the organization (see Argyris, 1964, and the literature

on self-governing work groups, e.g., Lysgaard, 1961) and industrial democracy (e.g., Dahlström, 1969; Karlsson, 1969; Thorsrud & Emery,
1964). These contributions, which are all closely related to administrative
theory, might be termed un-Weberian in the sense that they concentrate
almost exclusively on relationships and problems internal to the organization.
On this basis, Sunesson (1973, 1974) emphatically rejects "organization
theory" as historically uninformed and macrosociologically naive. He further
claims that Weber's intention in developing the concept of bureaucracy

> was not "organizational sociology" in any sense of the word, but was associ-
> ated with assumptions about a dominating *type of state,* i.e., a capitalist state,
> and an organizational system naturally related to it. Thus for Weber, the
> concept of "bureaucracy" was closely connected to a definite historical pro-
> cess. (Sunesson, 1974, p. 5, chap. 2)

This interpretation, I believe, makes a travesty of Weber's work. Admit-
tedly, modern organizational sociology deals with perspectives that by
Weberian standards are indeed somewhat narrow. But one may justify such
restricted approaches as a logical means for fulfilling Weber's intentions
when he formulated his concept of the ideal-typical bureaucracy. That is
to say, these organizational sociologists simply utilize Weber's formulation as a point of departure from which to proceed on a path that fulfills
the spirit of Weber's notion of bureaucracy. Weber examined bureaucracy
as a form of organization especially suited for, and functionally adapted
to, an economically developed, technically complex modern society. It is
from this point that modern organizational sociology departs and subsequently explores the logical extensions of Weber's work. For example,
modern social scientists often use Weber's framework to discuss and
analyze various types of organization and their relationship to efficiency.
Weber's concept of bureaucracy is a *construct,* a unit of comparison, an
idealized norm against which different forms of organization can be
compared and contrasted and against which deviations can be measured.
The Weberian ideal type has prepared the foundation for an organizational
sociology on the microlevel, a science of organization that no longer must
begin with an all-encompassing analysis of the total society, a science of
organization that does not need to resort to deliberations concerning the
character of the state and the social order.

The practical consequences of Weber's analysis of bureaucracy have
been considerable. He made it a legitimate undertaking to look at bureaucracy as a general phenomenon and not as something unique to state
administration. Through him, and the somewhat less influential Michels,
the groundwork was prepared for the "anatomical," microdirected analysis

of organizations, the application of which is the science of administration (see part II). One may regret the fact that in this process, organizational analysis has turned away from certain classical perspectives, but one can hardly maintain that this is un-Weberian. That is to say, Weber's analysis does *not* imply that it is necessary to connect the research on bureaucracy with research on the state and perhaps not even with macrorelations, because we have seen that he himself made use of innerlogical explanations.

Furthermore, Weber's theory of bureaucracy does *not* say that the concept of bureaucracy has to be tied to the *capitalist* order of production, as Sunesson (1974) maintains. It is true that Weber explained the emergence of bureaucracy by reference to the nature of the capitalist system but, as we have seen, Weber referred to this as merely *one of several* causal factors. Indeed, bureaucracies might well exist in societal forms *other* than those of the capitalistic world. Weber (1968) pointed to the *interconnection* between a capitalist economy and bureaucracy: "On the one hand, capitalism in its modern stages of development requires the bureaucracy, though both have arisen from different historical sources. Conversely, capitalism is the most rational economic basis for bureaucratic administration and enables it to develop in the most rational form" (p. 224). But Weber also argued that even if capitalism were abolished, bureaucracy would nonetheless remain. Thus he states in one of his political writings during World War I:

A progressive elimination of private capitalism is theoretically conceivable, although it is surely not so easy as imagined in the dreams of some literati who do not know what it is all about; its elimination will certainly not be a consequence of this war. But let us assume that some time in the future it will be done away with. What would be the practical result? The destruction of the steel frame of modern industrial work? No! The abolition of private capitalism would simply mean that also the *top management* of the nationalized or socialized enterprises would become bureaucratic. Are the daily working conditions of the salaried employees and the workers in the state-owned Prussian mines and railroads really perceptibly different from those in big business enterprises? It is true that there is even less freedom, since every power struggle with the state bureaucracy is hopeless and since there is no appeal to an agency which as a matter of principle would be interested in limiting the employer's power, such as there is in the case of a private enterprise. *That* would be the whole difference.

State bureaucracy would rule *alone* if private capitalism were eliminated. The private and public bureaucracies, which now work next to, and potentially against, each other, and hence check one another to a degree, would be merged into a single hierarchy. This would be similar to the situation in ancient Egypt, but it would occur in a much more rational—and hence unbreakable—form. (Weber, 1968, pp. 1401-1402)

It is obvious that Weber disliked such a development and that he saw bureaucracy in a society based on socialist economy as becoming a monolithic, immovable structure. In his early works as well, Weber portrayed bureaucracy as being independent of the economic system once it had been established. To Weber (1968), the indispensability of bureaucracy is a fact in all industrially developed societies: "It makes no difference whether the economic system is organized on a capitalistic or a socialistic basis" (p. 223).

A misconception similar to Sunesson's (1973, 1974) appears in Poulantzas's (1975) book *Political Power and Social Classes.* Poulantzas (1975) argues that Weber, along with the Marxist classics, "establishes a necessary relation between bureaucratism/bureaucracy and the capitalist mode of production" (p. 342). However, against the background of the quotation from Weber above, this certainly cannot be correct. Weber established a sufficient and not a necessary, relationship between bureaucracy and capitalism. Wherever capitalism flourishes, bureaucracy emerges. However, bureaucracy can also emerge, or continue to exist, under other conditions, e.g. socialism.

The Autonomy of Bureaucracy

A basic trait in Weber's theory is that it gives bureaucracy the character of an *impersonal apparatus* whose existence is motivated by technical competence, predictability of action, precision, stability, etc. In this sense, bureaucracy allows an exceptionally high degree of calculability (Weber, 1968, pp. 223-224). The loyalty of the official is not paid to any particular person, as in traditional or charismatic organizations, but rather, to the impersonal and functional purposes of the organization itself. The official is characterized by "a specific duty of fealty to the purpose of the office *(Amtstreue)*" (p. 959; cf. p. 988).

It is especially clear in Weber's (1968) article "Parliament and Government in a Reconstructed Germany" that he wanted to depict bureaucracy as a *machine,* perhaps an animated machine, but nevertheless as a structure based on "objectified intelligence."

An inanimate machine is mind objectified. Only this provides it with the power to force men into its service and to dominate their everyday working life as completely as is actually the case in the factory. Objectified intelligence is also that animated machine, the bureaucratic organization, with its specialization of trained skills, its division of jurisdiction, its rules and hierarchical relations of authority. (Weber, 1968, p. 1402)

After such a statement, one may feel that the answer to the question of whether bureaucracy can be an autonomous political force should be easy. Similar formulations appear in other writings by Weber. For example, in a description of modern capitalist industrial enterprise, he noted that to be run properly it would presuppose a bureaucracy, a legal and administrative system, the function of which may be predicted "by virtue of its fixed general norms, just like the expected performance of a machine" (Weber, 1968, p. 1394).

If bureaucracy is indeed a machine, it must be tended to. Someone must program it, give it proper tasks, lubricate it, and if necessary, repair it (i.e., issue new rules and regulations) and replace parts that are worn out or that no longer function properly (i.e., dismiss and hire personnel). It seems virtually impossible that Weber could have perceived bureaucracy as an autonomous social unit. The question, then, regarding control of the bureaucracy seems rather easy to answer: Bureaucracy subordinates itself to anyone who is able to master the economic and legal techniques necessary for its proper functioning.

It is easy to find statements by Weber (1968, p. 953) that support this contention. For example, Weber makes a clear distinction between *super-ordinates* (i.e., the masters) and *apparatus* (i.e., the bureaucracy). He argued that the "objective indispensability" of the bureaucratic "mechanism" makes it easy to get it to work "for anybody who knows how to gain control over it" (p. 988). The coup d'état, and not the revolution, becomes the typical means for obtaining control over the leadership of the state. Bureaucracy cannot be disposed of (p. 224), and therefore, groups in revolt need only to *take over* the previous machinery to successfully gain control. Those who seize this power may need to replace various top officials (p. 989), but thereafter, the bureaucracy is prepared to serve its new masters. It is able to serve any interest.

> [One has to remember] that bureaucracy as such is a precision instrument which can put itself at the disposal of quite varied interests, purely political as well as purely economic ones, or any other sort. (Weber, 1968, p. 990)

Even though Weber's standpoint may, to a certain extent, resemble that of Marxism in that they both stress bureaucracy's subordination to its masters, I feel that it is the differences between the two systems that is most striking. For example, Marx and Lenin emphasized bureaucracy's dependence on and attachments to the bourgeois state. Weber, on his part, energetically and eloquently stressed that the masters of bureaucracy may be motivated by *any* interests. Be these interests bourgeois or socialist, state or private, the bureaucracy will obediently follow their orders. Lenin, following Marx, emphasized that the proletariat's taking of power requires that the state apparatus be crushed. For Weber, shifts of power were merely a question of replacing a few public servants at the top of the hierarchy. (Compare Kautsky's argument in the dispute with Pannekoek, see Lenin, n.d.-a, pp. 103-111. Kautsky argued that the gaining of socialist power should not have as its purpose the abolishment of the state functions and dismissal of public officials, since these officials would be needed for the reconstruction of the new society. Nor should the state departments be dissolved. Lenin's standpoint was that such departments should be replaced by expert commissions and Soviets of workers and soldiers.)

However, Weber's opinion on the question of bureaucratic autonomy and the possibilities for bureaucracy exerting power on its own cannot, and should not, be summarized in such a simple way as I have done here. It is evident that he was ambiguous in regard to this issue, and that he could see the possibility of a bureaucratic machine revolting against its masters. The reason for this can be found in the fact that bureaucracies possess superior technical and practical knowledge as well as the ability to dominate the gathering and dissemination of vital information. "Bureaucratic administration means fundamentally domination through knowledge" (Weber, 1968, p. 225).

The notion that bureaucracy *has* power due to the fact that knowledge *is* power, is clearly in line with Weber's general view that power is controlled by *individuals*. As one commentator has pointed out (Sunesson, 1974, p. 22), social institutions are seen by Weber as a form of aggregated action. The power of bureaucracy becomes an expression of accumulated administrative knowledge transformed into praxis. Such influence may be exerted against the superordinate of the bureaucratic system and against the organization's environment. That is, to the extent that the bureaucracy has interests of its own, the possibility exists that this knowledge will be used in a way that is beneficial, first, to the group of bureaucrats, and only second, if at all, to its mandators. In his general theory of bureaucracy, Weber was not sure as to how much power bureaucracy is actually able to command. What he evidently meant, however, was that it is not possible to off-handedly predict such behavior.

> It must also remain an open question whether the *power* of bureaucracy is increasing in the modern states in which it is spreading. The fact that bureaucratic organization is technically the most highly developed power instrument in the hands of its controller does not determine the weight that bureaucracy as such is capable of procuring for its own opinions in a particular social structure. (Weber, 1968, p. 991)

Perhaps the best summary of Weber's view on the power of bureaucracy is to say that its influence is contingent on the specific circumstances present. *If* bureaucracy chooses to act politically its masters could easily become victims, since they lack the necessary expertise to effectively control the reigns of the bureaucracy. It is easier for the career official to pursue his opinion vis-à-vis the chief of state than it is for the official's nominal superior, i.e., the cabinet minister (Weber, 1968, p. 224). This is due to the simple fact that the latter lacks the adequate know-how. The superordinates of the bureaucracy are always (note the word) subordinated in relationship to experienced officials, the superordinate playing the role of a "dilettante facing the expert" (p. 991). This is regardless of who the superordinate is: the general public, the parliament, etc.

The bureaucrat may keep information secret if he or she finds this suitable for his or her purposes. Weber points to the example of Prussia where public statistics existed, but where only those data that were harmless to bureaucracy were made public. Bureaucracy dislikes public scrutiny. "Bureaucracy naturally prefers a poorly informed, and hence powerless, parliament—at least insofar as this ignorance is compatible with the bureaucracy's own interests" (Weber, 1968, p. 993) Here, Weber becomes unusually categorical. "*Against* the bureaucracy the ruler remains powerless" (p. 993).

One possible explanation for Weber's fuzziness on the issue of the power of bureaucracy is that he concentrated so strongly on the studies of the *character* and *inner properties* of bureaucracy that he came to overlook the issue of the *conditions* for bureaucratic insubordination. However, a qualification to this statement must be made. He did, at least in one case, explicitly bring up the problem of the power of bureaucracy. It was in reference to the situation in Germany immediately after World War I, and in this particular instance he was pointedly clear about the fact that bureaucracy had developed a power position of its own. The main cause of this, as he saw it, was that the parliament lacked the ability to supervise the administration. The state officials could not be subjected to public questioning (Weber, 1968, p. 1418), and the actions of the administration were not subject to inspection (pp. 1418-1419). After Bismarck's resignation, Germany was ruled by bureaucrats with the result that all political talent was eliminated. Openness, elimination of "official secrets" and the introduction of effective parliamentary control were necessary for reducing the influence of the bureaucracy to its rightful proportions. As conditions were, the system allowed "qualified bureaucrats who nevertheless have no traits of statesman-like talent to maintain themselves in leading political positions until some intrigue forces them out in favor of similar personages" (Weber, 1968, p. 1410).

The Elimination of Bureaucracy

On this point, Weber is exceptionally clear. He felt that, from a technical viewpoint, the bureaucratic type of administration is indeed capable of reaching the maximum degree of efficiency (Weber, 1968, p. 223). Thereby it is "the most rational known means of exercising authority over human beings" (p. 223). It is fruitless to try to avoid bureaucracy. The only choice is between bureaucracy and dilettantism. To fight bureaucracy one needs bureaucracy. "When those subject to bureaucratic control seek to escape the influence of the existing bureaucratic apparatus, this is normally possible only by creating an organization of their own which is equally subject to bureaucratization" (p. 224).

That the existence of bureaucracy means definite problems in the implementation of democracy is certainly unquestionable. As organizations emerge and grow large, a bureaucratic administration becomes necessary, hindering direct democracy from being practiced. In whatever organization it exists, direct democracy becomes unstable in that there always exists a tendency for the resourceful to take over the administrative functions for their own purposes (Weber, 1968, p. 949). It is, however, theoretically conceivable to dispose of bureaucracy by returning to a social system composed of very small organizations (p. 224), yet it is evident that Weber did not see this as a real alternative. While bureaucracy *can* be controlled under certain circumstances through parliament,[11] the contradiction between democracy and bureaucratic rule nonetheless appears to be permanent (p. 991).

Robert Michels: The Natural Law of Power Concentration

At a quick glance, it may seem that Michels does not belong in this discussion. Michels primarily wrote about tendencies toward the concentration of power and minority rule; in explicit words, he only superficially dealt with bureaucracy, and then only as a concept that can be equated with state administration. But the discussion on Michels's (1958) most important contribution, *Political Parties,* is still quite relevant. As it was first issued in Germany in 1911, Michels's book may be seen as a parallel to Weber's treatment of the emergence of bureaucracy. Whereas the size and complexity of an organization is emphasized in Weber's work as a *contributing* cause of its bureaucratization, these factors assume a far greater importance in Michels's theory. Both the originality and the limitations of Michels's (1958) treatment of oligarchic tendencies stem from his almost manic attachment to, and purification of, the thesis of the inevitability of oligarchic tendencies, "the iron law of oligarchy" (pp. 393-409). It is original in that the mechanisms of the deformation of power in big organizations have not by any previous social scientist been given such a significant formulation. Its limitations are due to Michels's hardheaded fixation on his basic thesis. By doing so, he establishes an effective block to any deliberation of how oligarchic tendencies might possibly be modified.

When Michels talks of oligarchy, he comes very close to the explication of the essence of bureaucracy that I have tried to make in Chapter 1. As he intended to show, Michels's law of oligarchy is an expression of the inevitable and unrestrained tendency that the conflicts between the demands of efficiency and democracy are always solved to the advantage of those forces acting on behalf of efficiency, and therefore at the cost of democracy. There is strong reason to emphasize the term *forces,* since Michels has often been misunderstood. His exposition of oligarchical tendencies has sometimes been seen as a description of how leading strata political organizations consciously, and as part of a personal striving for power, try to consolidate and reinforce their positions. This is only partially correct. The dominating characteristic of Michels's book is the dogged stressing of the *necessity* and the *regularity* of something that is built *into the organizational principle itself.* Oligarchy irresistibly follows from people's attempts to organize in associations and unions. *Political Parties* is written partly as a polemic against those who believe that oligarchy can be avoided. For example, Michels (1958) triumphantly points to the fact that the first workers' organizations in Germany, Allgemeiner Deutscher Arbeiterverein, was ruled autocratically by Ferdinand Lassalle, who made use of "a power comparable with that of the doge of the Venetian Republic" (p. 201). Furthermore, the general assembly of the First International was subordinated to "the iron will of one single man, Karl Marx" (p. 204). The International, according to Michels, was seen by many as the negation of socialism because it introduced the authority principle into workers' politics.

Michels major polemical point is his demonstration that the tendencies toward power concentration are significant characteristics even in organizations that have very explicit democratic goals. His foremost example is that of the German Social Democratic Party, but he also takes great pains to show that syndicalism, as well as anarchism, are not immune to the tendencies toward oligarchy (1958, part V, chaps. 3-4).

On the rare occasions when the term *bureaucracy* appears in Michels's work, it is used as a label for the officials employed by the state and the political organizations. Both the state and the political parties try to acquire as broad a base as possible. As an element of this policy, they recruit a great number of administrators, who because of their economic dependence on the organization, act for their benefit. Thus not only do the state and political organizations need administrators but the creation of big administrations is the functional answer to the career needs of many intellectuals. Another demand for extensive administration arises because of the large number of tasks that the modern organization needs to perform. Here Michels (1958, p. 196) refers back to his general discussion about the causes of oligarchy.

Michels's section on bureaucracy is clearly subordinated to his general theory of oligarchy, and it is obvious that Michels views bureaucracy as only one element in the concentration of power and influence within a small stratum of leaders. In Michels's (1958) *Political Parties* both *oligarchy* and *bureaucracy* are terms generally used to represent *elite rule.*

The Emergence of Elite Rule

Leadership, says Michels, is a necessary phenomenon of all social life. It is pointless to ask whether it is a good or bad phenomenon. All that science can do is to establish the law of the inevitability of oligarchy, and then to try to determine and explain the causes of oligarchic tendencies (Michels, 1958, p. 418). Wherever we encounter organization, we find oligarchy as well.

> *Organization implies the tendency to oligarchy.* In every organization, whether it be a political party, a professional union, or any other association of the kind, the aristocratic tendency manifests itself very clearly. . . . *As a result of organization,* every party or professional union becomes divided into a minority of directors and a majority of directed. (Michels, 1958, p. 37; emphasis added)

> *Who says organization, says oligarchy.* (p. 418; emphasis added)

Michels's line of reasoning is close to the thinking of elite theoreticians such as Mosca and Pareto. In partial resemblance to them, especially to Pareto, he attributes some of the causes for the emergence of elite rule to psychological factors of the upwardly mobile strata. Oligarchy stems from the psychological transformations of the leading personalities within the parties. In contrast to the other elite theoreticians, however, Michels also carefully surveys a number of internal organizational variables, such as factors connected with tactical and technical necessities. This survey, in turn, becomes part of a debate against those utopians, primarily socialists, who believe that direct democracy and broad membership participation is possible in a political organization. The tactical and technical factors that are mentioned by Michels as reasons for the development of an elite stratum and that subsequently make direct democracy impossible are the following:

A. The *number* of members. To organize meetings in which up to 1,000 members participate is highly difficult, says Michels (1958), "especially in northern climes, where the weather makes it impossible to hold open-air meetings for the greater part of the year" (p. 30). Furthermore, no speaker can make himself or herself heard to more than 10,000 members, "even if we imagine the means of communication to become much better than those which now exist" (p. 31). Note that in just a few years this statement was to be profoundly falsified because of radio communications.

B. The need to decide on *matters of dispute* among members. Controversies between two parties within the organization cannot be settled by participation of the entire collective in the process (Michels, 1958, p. 31).

This leads to a need for a system of delegation, i.e., a system in which appointed persons represent the mass of members and execute their will. This need for delegation also arises from every organization's need for:

C. *Expertise.* The technical specialization that inevitably results from large-scale organization creates the need for a staff of experts. In referring to Heinrich Herkner's (1908) *Die Arbeiterfrage,* Michels (1958) also stresses the fact that the workers' organizations are forced toward professionalization because of their having to defend themselves against the expert power which the employers' organizations are able to mobilize, their employees being "university men" (p. 33; cf. pp. 38-39).

There is another factor, however, which is perhaps more important still. In work conflicts and strikes, the rapid mobilization of the collective forces of the organization becomes a necessity. According to Lassalle, the organization should be able to act like a "hammer" in the hands of its leadership. Thus the concentration of executive power is needed to allow for:

D. *Quick decisions.* The modern party is a fighting organization and requires a certain degree of "caesarism" if orders are to be quickly communicated and executed (Michels, 1958, p. 48). Michels points out the similarities between an actively fighting political party and a military organization and points to the irony in the military terminology he finds in the writings of leading German socialists, e.g., Kautsky.

Finally, there exists a vast mobility in the membership cadres of political organizations, which gives rise to the need for:

E. *Continuity* in the leadership of the organization. Particularly in the trade unions, the mobility of members is considerable. To preserve continuity, a leadership stratum is required that can form "a more stable and more constant element of the organized membership" (Michels, 1958, p. 85).

It is not entirely clear what Michels means when he speaks of "psychological factors" leading to oligarchy, but the examples he provides seem to point to the existence of certain permanent character traits both among the members and those in leadership positions.

A. As soon as a delegate is elected, Michels (1958) says, he tends to perceive his post as a lifetime appointment, as his "property" (p. 50). For this reason, organizations that take care to appear especially democratic try to introduce rules concerning short mandate periods (p. 103). But tradition, the need for stability, and sometimes the leaders' own threats to abdicate often lead to a permanence for such positions.

B. There is a born leader in every good speaker and journalist, Michels says. The oratoric quality of a political leader in a democracy is an extremely strong force in the direction of power concentration: "The essential characteristic of democracy is found in the readiness with which it succumbs to the magic of words, written as well as spoken" (Michels, 1958, p. 75).

C. The most important of these psychological factors has to do with the idea that members in an organization experience a need for a leader. Most people are politically detached. The decisions made within a party are always made by a small handful of members, with the majority of the members being satisfied with participation in the political elections (Michels, 1958, pp. 54-55). The majority usually appreciates the fact that there are persons who want to devote their time to represent its interests (p. 58).

In Michels's treatment of the relationship between oligarchical tendencies and psychological factors, one can easily discover his basic assumptions about human nature. They are, to be sure, pessimistic: Egoism, particularism, and a quest for material gains are strong driving forces behind the decisions of people who go into politics (Michels, 1958, pp. 54-55). The mass can never gain influence over an organization because it is amorphous and incompetent, therefore needing a distribution of labor, specialization, and leadership (p. 421). "Man as individual is by nature predestined to be guided, and to be guided all the more in proportion as the functions of life undergo division and subdivision" (p. 422). As a rule, the contradiction between democratic and aristocratic processes in organizations tends to be solved in favor of the aristocracy.

The contrast between Michels's viewpoints and, for example, either John Stuart Mill's view of democracy or the classical Marxist perception of bureaucracy and the problems of administration, could hardly be greater. Mill emphasizes the importance of everyone participating in the organization and, as an essential criterion of democracy, everyone being *trained* to protect their interests. Through this process the individual's responsibility for the totality is developed. Similarly, Marx and Lenin are optimistic about the possibilities of implementing broad participation in the leadership of the state, once the old state apparatus has been abolished. To Michels (1958, p. 420), however, such a hope is vain. He contends that socialists are wrong when they maintain that the difficulties of democracy stem from the fact that the masses, in earlier epochs, were repressed through slavery and exploitation. Oligarchic tendencies are always present and, therefore, cannot be attributed to any particular epoch. Consequently, they cannot be abolished through social transformation in the form of a revolution.

The Autonomy of the Ruling Elite

In discussing Michels's view of the autonomy of the executive stratum, it is necessary to differentiate between the *employed* and the *elected* executive. The employed executive, or bureaucracy, is viewed by Michels as a subordinate category, strongly dependent on its masters. For example, the state bureaucracy takes on as its task the defense of the state in exchange for economic remuneration as well as the security offered by the state.

Public officials are dependent on their superordinates (Michels, 1958, p. 200). The possibility that bureaucracy might revolt against its masters is not within the framework of Michels's theory. Such an omission is easily understandable. Since his theses concern tendencies toward concentration of power in the *political* leadership, i.e., the elected executive, he has to avoid giving the impression that such monolithic power can be shaken or counteracted by actions from other groups. (This problem resembles the difficulties found within the Marxist conception of bureaucracy when it confronts the possibility of an autonomous stratum of public servants; see "Autonomy of the Bureaucracy," above). In passing, however, Michels takes care to note some dysfunctional tendencies of bureaucracy. For example, it is hostile to initiative, it represses individuality, it replaces goals with means, it leads to moral poverty, etc. Thus Michels carries out an analysis that in many respects anticipates Merton's (1957) well-known article "Bureaucratic Structure and Personality" (see Michels, 1958, pp. 198-199).

The Elimination of Elite Rule

I have already reviewed the major aspects of Michels's viewpoint in regard to the possibilities of eliminating tendencies to oligarchy. Simply put, they are that organization implies oligarchy and that organization without immanent tendencies of elite formation are unimaginable. In short, elite rule cannot be abolished.

Despite the fact that Michels's main thesis is expressed quite emphatically, it would be incorrect to give the impression that he does not discuss at all how oligarchic tendencies may be modified. In the last pages of his book, he actually shows a degree of reverence for democracy, albeit in a very restricted manner. He feels that democratic movements are not completely ineffectual in checking the tendencies toward elite rule. Even if such movements never "discover" democracy, they nonetheless carry out valuable work during their search for it (Michels, 1958, p. 423). For example, the workers' movements strengthen and stimulate the intellectual abilities of the individuals involved, along with their abilities to criticize and control, characteristics which may be further improved by education (p. 424). Michels's modifications, however, are presented in an abrupt and abbreviated manner, thus acquiring the character of quickly improvised qualifications. Through them, he tries to attenuate the rather doomsdaylike forecast he has created in the rest of his book. The lasting impression of Michels's major work, however, is that democracy appears to be, for the most part, completely lacking in the ability to check the automatic, natural-law forces of oligarchy.

Discussion

I have already pointed out that it seems impossible to reconcile the various conceptualizations of bureaucracy that have been reviewed above. True, they have certain important aspects in common. (1) They deal with the same problem in that they work with the two conflicting goals of administrative efficiency and effective representation. (2) They have in common in their descriptive parts the treatment of different issues that pertain to the administrative system of organizations.

With these two similarities exhausted, the contrasts become the dominating features. There is a sharp confrontation between the classical Marxist view of bureaucracy, on the one hand, and Michels's theory of oligarchic processes, on the other. Both theories raise large, even absolutistic claims. The former maintains that the analysis of bureaucracy cannot be separated from the analysis of capitalist society and the state. That is, bureaucracy is the official servant of capitalism, thus the characteristics of bureaucracy are dependent on the bourgeois state. The latter theory categorically holds that organization in itself leads to oligarchy. Rule of the few and the transference of power from the original mandators of the organization to a small circle of leaders is immanent in the organization principle. Thus the theory of bureaucracy as dependent on specific *external forces* is contrasted to the theory of bureaucracy as a general organizational phenomenon stemming from *inner processes* in the organization. If one accepts the former, one must reject the latter, and vice versa.

My thesis in this final section is that neither the Marxist view of bureaucracy nor Michels's theory of immanence contains adequate explanations of the emergence and development of bureaucracy. Nevertheless, the two theories form perspectives that, precisely because of their contradictory natures, increase the fruitfulness of the analysis of bureaucracy. To a large degree, the two perspectives have been brought together in a kind of compromise by Weber. To Weber, bureaucracy is contingent both on structural-macroscopic processes *and* on the internal processes within organizations. The latter, however, cannot be isolated from the former. What happens within organizations in the last instance is dependent on forces in the surrounding society. This does not necessarily imply that a study of a certain organization has to start with a comprehensive societal analysis, however.

In which ways are the Marxist and Michelsian theories problematic? I shall briefly try to mention some of the major arguments in the following two sections.

The Marxist Concept of Bureaucracy: Bureaucracy Associated With the Bourgeois State

The problems that arise in the Marxist view of bureaucracy can best be demonstrated by giving three different emphases to the thesis in the heading above, i.e., (1) the association of bureaucracy with the bourgeois *state,* (2) the association of bureaucracy with the *bourgeois* state, and (3) *the association* of bureaucracy *with* the bourgeois state.

The Association of Bureaucracy With the Bourgeois *State*

If one argues that bureaucracy is a phenomenon that is tied exclusively to the administration of the state, it becomes difficult to explain in *other* organizations the tendencies of growing hierarchy, expert rule, systems of privileges, and increasing rigidity. As we have seen, Lenin's solution is to refer to the demoralizing impact of the capitalist environment when such tendencies of bureaucracy emerge in trade unions and political organizations. In their case, then, bureaucracy can be explained by pointing to the characteristics of bourgeois society. There does not exist in the classical Marxist tradition any particular theory of bureaucracy for organizations other than the state.

One reasonable explanation for the weakness of Marxist theory on this point is provided by Berntson (1974) in his book *Political Parties and Social Classes* (*Politiska partier och sociala klasser*). Marxism is a theory

for the analysis of social structure and class relationships on macrolevel
and intermediate level, and it is not—at least in the form it was given by
Marx, Lenin, Engels, and later Poulantzas—a theory for the explanation
of phenomena on a microlevel (i.e., organizations, small groups, individuals). To exemplify this, a natural application of Marxist organizational
analysis would be to study political parties. Berntson (1974) notes, however, that the study of these organizations "are outside the traditional
object of historical materialism" (p. 18). Thus Berntson (1974) takes on
the task of filling in the theoretical holes left by the Marxist tradition in
the field of organization theory. He does this by analyzing the internal
conditions of political parties against the background of the broader social
theory and the theory of class relations.[12]

The Association of Bureaucracy With the *Bourgeois* State

How does classical Marxism explain the presence of bureaucracy after
the revolution has been carried out? The theory may be resorted to in this
case as well, since bureaucracy can be shown once to have constituted an
integral part of capitalist society. If that society was inadequately developed, this fact provides further support for the notion that bureaucracy
rests on the remnants of previous societal formations. The bourgeois
repression apparatus had been destroyed, Lenin (n.d.-b) said in 1919, but
the need for a state apparatus remained: "Here we are suffering from the
fact that Russia was not sufficiently developed capitalistically." The bourgeois state with its mechanisms of administration and distribution was able
to survive partly because of bureaucratic "elements."

The explanation is risky, however, since it implies that bureaucracy will
in fact gradually decrease following the development of the productive
forces in the socialist society. If this were in fact the case, one would
expect that increased economic development, public education, etc., in a
socialist society would be accompanied by an attenuation and gradual
dissolution of the system of bureaucratic privileges. The fact that this did
not take place was the basis of the critique by Trotsky and the leftist
opposition to Stalin's growing power during the 1920s. According to the
established party functionaries, explained Trotsky (1923/1972), "bureaucratism was nothing else than a leftover from the war period, i.e., a
phenomenon in the process of dying away" (p. 17). But according to
Trotsky (1923/1972) himself, bureaucratism is a phenomenon that stems
from factors *within* the apparatus.

> The state apparatus is the most important source of bureaucratism. On the one
> hand, it sips off an enormous amount of the most active elements of the party

and educates the most competent group among these in the administration of people and things, and not in the political leadership of the masses. On the other hand, it must be paid great attention to by the party apparatus, and in this sense can exert influence because of its administrative methods. (p. 39)

The party was living at two different levels: "the top floor where things are decided on, and the ground floor where decisions are received and obeyed" (Trotsky, 1923/1972, p. 16).

Trotsky's argument resembles Michels's discussion in that it directs our attention to the inner mechanisms and tendencies of deformation in the state apparatus. However, there are two modifications of this statement that need to be made. First, Trotsky and his followers generally agreed with the theory that emphasized the primary role of the economy for the elimination of bureaucracy within the state and party machinery (i.e., an improvement of the economy would lead to, among other things, increased education). Second, Trotsky expanded the scope of his thesis when he stated that the Soviet Union was dependent on the spread of revolution to other countries and when he denied the possibility of "socialism in one country."

Both Trotsky's critique and Michels's discussion of oligarchy highlight the fact that an explanation of bureaucracy in terms of its dependence on a certain kind of society or state is not adequate. Such a macroanalysis often requires a complement in the form of assumptions regarding immanent processes.

The *Association* of Bureaucracy *With* the Bourgeois State

It is possible that certain Marxists reject theories of inner logic because such theories make it more difficult to wed the problems of bureaucracy with the characteristics of the capitalist society. Take, for example, Sunesson (1973), who objects to the "general interpretations of the problem of bureaucracy made by L. Trotsky and bourgeois historicist elite theoreticians like Robert Michels" (p. 9). He attacks "the texts by the so-called Trotsky-ites" for dealing with the problem of bureaucracy as "separated from history, as a general organizational problem" (p. 6).

If the ideas of inner logic are accepted, one cannot theoretically rule out the possibility that a bureaucratic stratum will arise as a natural consequence in a society based even on socialist principles. This recognition of the possibilities of an autonomous bureaucratic power center means that the door is open to possible accusations that the existing state and party apparatus actually *is* such a center of power. Such a recognition represents a fundamental flaw in the *theory,* because it makes the hypothesis about the polarization of society into two antagonistic classes less credible. That is, if the possibility of an autonomous bureaucracy is acknowledged, it also becomes possible that bureaucracy in a certain society may become, or has already become, a new class.

If, on the other hand, such autonomy is accepted as possible, difficulties arise on several issues when the theory is confronted with reality. The military coup in Chile might be explained as an example of the power strivings of capitalism (the bourgeoisie, or U.S. imperialism) and not primarily as a military coup (see editorial in *Häften för Kritiska Studier,* no. 7, 1973), but can the same model be applied to other revolts by the military? Does the military always act as an agent of the ruling class? For example, the events in Portugal after Salazar led to the legalization of the Communist party, the acceptance of strikes and unions, the increased influence of Socialists and Communists in the government, and the initiation of negotiation of independence with the African resistance movements in the Portuguese colonies. Certain interest groups in industry might have condoned the military coup because they saw both the possibility of a decrease in colonial military expenses and an increase in the accessibility to investment capital (*Dagens Nyheter,* May 17, 1974), but it is hard to see that the coup could have been particularly welcomed by the major part of the dominating power groups, who immediately lost the support they had been able to gain from the previous government (under Caetano). Therefore, it seems that, to a large degree, the military revolt in Portugal can be explained by the particular grievances in the military itself.

The Marxist may object that the military revolt in Portugal is rather an example of what Poulantzas calls the "relative autonomy" of a bureaucratic group within "the capitalist class state." Which role does this class state play, according to Poulantzas (1975)?

> It can be stated as follows: it takes charge, as it were, of the bourgeoisie's political interests and realizes the function of political hegemony which the bourgeoisie is unable to achieve. But *in order to do this, the capitalist state assumes a relative autonomy with regard to the bourgeoisie.* This is why Marx's analyses of Bonapartism as a capitalist type of state are so significant. For this relative autonomy allows the state to intervene not only in order to arrange compromises vis-à-vis the dominating classes, which, in the long run, are useful for the actual economic interests of the dominant classes or fractions; but also (dependent on the concrete conjuncture) to intervene against the long-term economic interests of *one or other* fraction of the dominant class: for such compromises and sacrifices are sometimes necessary for the realization of their political class interests. (pp. 284-285)

The employment of the concept of relative autonomy is motivated by the ambition of correcting "a simplistic and vulgarized conception which sees in the state the tool or instrument of the dominant class" (Poulantzas, 1975, p. 256). Bureaucracy, says Poulantzas, is also characterized by "relative autonomy," "by its character as a specific category through the intermediary of its relation with the state" (p. 337).

The term *relative autonomy* is a good safety valve for the Marxist theory of bureaucracy, since almost any action by a group or stratum might be explained as being advantageous to the interests of the bourgeoisie. Anyway, what can*not* be shown to be a "compromise" in "the long run" if only the run is long enough? Furthermore, Poulantzas does not give any example of when and how these interests would not be supported, thus giving the theory an empty and empirically untestable quality, due to the fact that the limits of his relative autonomy are not indicated. (I suppose that Poulantzas means that a socialist revolution would transcend these limits, but there are a lot of other possible threats against the interests of the bourgeoisie on which it would have been interesting to have his opinion.)

Sunesson (1974) argues in the same vague and imprecise manner in his discussion about "concessions made by the state" (p. 89). The state allows "certain economic concessions" to reinforce the political interests of the capitalist class in the long run. This may be so. However, the interesting problem is to discuss in which concrete case a real, and for capitalism harmful, concession actually is being made by the state.

There is further reason to raise the question as to what extent Poulantzas actually brings about any modification of the *instrument thesis* in Marxism. Like Lenin, Poulantzas contends that bureaucracy has to be analyzed, as a matter of definition, in connection with the capitalist state. It is symptomatic of his position that he bluntly rejects, on a theoretical basis, the hypothesis about the possible autonomy of bureaucracy. When studying bureaucracy, he states, one has "no theoretical need to concede it its own political power" (Poulantzas, 1975, p. 337). Just like the state, bureaucracy is "simply the center of class power" (p. 337).

From the viewpoint of empirical research, such a strong aprioristic position does not seem too fruitful. Aside from its lack of testability, it carries the uncomfortable burden of the requirement that all actions by bureaucratic groups must be explained by referring to characteristics of the capitalist society. Poulantzas may have wanted to object by saying that the analysis of specific bureaucratic phenomena without making this broader reference may make us not see the forest because of all the trees. While recognizing the need for being aware of the forest—i.e., the social macroconditions—I feel that, on a good many occasions, trees (i.e., the specific actions of bureaucratic groups) can be pretty interesting in themselves.

A Note on Michels

For similar reasons, it is difficult to accept the whole of Michels's theory. To Michels, *all* organizations, regardless of type or inner structure, have tendencies toward oligarchic control, i.e., toward a differentiation between the leaders and the led. Two points should be stressed. First, Michels carries out his work on the basis of an implicit direct-democratic model. Because of this, every form of representative system and system of delegates can be taken as evidence that an oligarchy exists, and since each organization of any reasonable size has to have some kind of representative system, every organization thereby becomes oligarchic (on the need for delegation as a consequence of organizational size, see Abrahamsson, 1993, chap. 7).

Furthermore, Michels directs our attention primarily to the *form* of decision making and ignores the *content* of the decisions involved. It is quite possible that even a very small group in the leadership of the organization, because of good contacts with lower-level members, can reach decisions that are in accordance with the goals and interests of the mandators and participants.

The second point that should be stressed about Michels's theory is that it is virtually blind to the society that surrounds the organization, as well as to those historical processes that gave rise to the organizations initially. To Michels, there is no difference between the organizational *principle* on the one hand, and, on the other, a specific *organization.* Thus he takes no interest in investigating the conditions underlying the emergence and development of a certain association, nor does he question to what extent this emergence is dependent on economic, technological, and political-social forces. The reason for this is that he already has the answer. Elite formation tendencies are treated as "given" and can be explained partly by technical and tactical factors and partly by psychological factors connected with the leaders and the led.

Michels's argument is not altogether unaffected by his general polemics. *Political Parties* is only partially a social-scientific product, his general aim is the reduction of popular support for German Social Democracy (see also Abrahamsson, 1993, chap. 9).

The Synthesis: Max Weber

To a substantial degree, the concepts of bureaucracy set forth by Michels and the Marxists are integrated by the contributions of Weber. As we have seen, Weber's theory, first, connects the developments of bureaucracy with the issue of the long-run material and political development of society. The capitalistic production system and economy are two of the most important factors in Weber's explanatory scheme. In those respects, there are important similarities between Weber and the Marxist tradition. Second, Weber points to the importance of immanent organizational factors that move the organization toward bureaucratization. An especially important factor is the increase in size of organizations, which leads to a need for "mass administration" and that makes direct democracy impossible. In these microaspects, there are clear parallels between Weber and Michels.

I have questioned the possibility of integrating all theories of bureaucracy within a common frame of reference. But is Weber providing us with the roof under which Marx and Michels might feel at home? No. As the reader may recall, I said previously that one criterion of an integrative theory is its possibility to explain both bureaucratization and debureaucratization. Even though Weber, in his stress on macroaspects and in his broad historical survey, has very much in common with the Marxist tradition, he differs nonetheless in at least one major respect. Weber's theory is a theory about the impossibility of eliminating bureaucracy, whereas Marx's theory explicitly explains how this elimination can and will be accomplished. As has been stressed several times above, Weber also contradicts Marx's theory at another point: He leaves open the possibility that bureaucracy may act autonomously thereby rejecting the Marxist hypothesis of polarization.

The contrasts between Weber and Michels are less obvious. Like Michels, Weber is a generalist, i.e., he investigates bureaucracy as a *general* organizational phenomenon. There are also similarities between Michels's formulation of his thesis as a natural law, and Weber's way of explaining the bureaucratic ideal type as the end point of an administrative evolution. The contrasts only become evident when one looks at the specific groups of explanatory factors that the two authors emphasize. Despite the formal elegance and eloquence of Michels's theory, it appears as lacking in detail in comparison to the enormous scanning of the broad historical processes put forward by Weber. Weber deals with processes where psychological factors and the character traits of individuals play a rather subordinated role, and where the general development of organizations—their increasing size and inner differentiation along with their problems of government—are never completely isolated from the background drawings of economic and political conditions.

Notes

1. See T. M. Knox's (1942) translation of Hegel's *Philosophy of Right* (pp. 188-189).

2. See Håkanson (1973, pp. 158ff.). Håkanson's polemics against Gustafsson's introduction to *Socialkapitalismen* (Social Capitalism) is based on the distinction between bureaucratic structure and bureaucratic elements. One of Håkanson's arguments is that Gustafsson trivializes the content of a pamphlet by the Hungarian writer Varga (*The Russian Road to Socialism*) by ignoring that Varga gives *structural* reasons for the growth of bureaucracy under Stalin.

3. Germain (1969, p. 3)—who recognizes the possibility of general bureaucratization mechanisms and is thus not limited to bourgeois societies—uses the concept of workers' bureaucracy as a label of administrative deformations of socialist states and workers' organizations. Germain carries out an analysis of bureaucratization processes within the workers' movement that in many respects resembles Michels's discussion of oligarchic phenomena in *Political Parties*. Thus Germain points to the need of mass organizations for permanent administrative apparatuses, for the privileges that are usually attached to positions within these apparatuses, for the influence of experts, etc. (cf. Mandel, 1971: "Lenin to a great extent underestimated . . . the danger that the apparatus might become autonomous and the danger of bureaucratization of the workers' parties," p. 27).

Sunesson (1973) attacks Germain (Mandel) because the latter views the problem of bureaucracy as "separated from history, as a general organizational problem" (p. 6). This highlights the question of whether bureaucracy is an immanent organizational phenomenon (Michels) or whether its emergence is related to primarily external forces (e.g., the capitalist social order).

4. Lenin's determination of democracy contains various ambiguities and changes between the components of form and content. According to the quotation given here, the state "in its proper sense" will disappear when the proletariat takes power. However, as Håkanson (1973) points out, this takeover means that force still has to be asserted. The democracy sketched by Lenin is also a *state*. "It contains repression through means of violence. And in exactly the same way as the democratic republic within the framework of capitalism is democracy for the rich, the dictatorship of the proletariat is democracy for the proletariat with the exception of its previous repressors" (Håkanson,1973, p. 353). Håkanson feels that as long as there exists an apparatus of repression, democracy is not fulfilled because the exertion of force blocks the implementation of certain important socialist values.

Within the framework of this chapter it is not possible to account for the different aspects of Lenin's views on democracy, and even less possible to review the turns in the discussion of it. The reader is referred to Håkanson's (1973) detailed analysis of *The State and Revolution* (esp. pp. 107-110, chap. 7).

5. Markovic (1972, chap. 7) thinks that while the administrative tasks have become more complicated, modern science and technology, especially cybernetics, have opened up possibilities for the elimination of bureaucracy and the implementation of self-government.

6. See Håkanson (1973, pp. 80f.).

7. Håkanson (1973, pp. 321-322).

8. Albrow (1970, pp. 52-54) demonstrates Weber's strong dependence on Schmoller, who (in several papers in 1894 and 1898) put forward, first, an evolutionary theory about administrative forms and, second, sketched a final state of this development in terms that correspond almost detail by detail to the Weberian ideal type of bureaucracy.

9. For Weber's description of the bureaucratic ideal type, see the box.

10. This is stressed by Sunesson (1974) who goes on: "His [Weber's] theory is rather a kind of check list of phenomena which the sociologist is recommended to pay attention to" (p. 24).

11. Weber's enthusiasm for the parliamentary form of government was possibly more dependent on his "conviction that national greatness depended on finding able leaders than to any concern for democratic values" (Albrow, 1970, p. 49). "As early as 1895, in his inaugural lecture, Weber had taken 'national power' as a political good of paramount importance. The extent of Weber's nationalism and responsibility for later developments in Germany have become a matter for heated debate" (p. 131).

12. It is interesting to note that he tries to reconcile Marx with Parsons. Despite the criticism that Berntson (1974) advances against the action theory of Parsons, the latter is used to provide the explanations of these "subjective notions which rule the explicit action of political parties" (p. 36). To an outside observer, it would appear more natural if internal organization mechanisms were discussed and demonstrated by referring to Marxists like Trotsky, Mandel, and others. Remarkably, however, they are totally absent in Berntson's list of references.

PART II

ADMINISTRATION THEORY
Rationalism and the
Systems Perspective

3

Classical and Modern in Organization Theory

Dad took moving pictures of us children washing dishes, so that he could figure out how we could reduce our motions and thus hurry through the task. Irregular jobs, such as painting the back porch or removing a stump from the front lawn, were awarded on a low-bid basis. Each child who wanted extra pocket money submitted a sealed bid saying what he would do the job for. The lowest bidder got the contract. . . .

Yes, at home or on the job, Dad was always the efficiency expert. He buttoned his vest from the bottom up, instead of from the top down, because the bottom-to-top process took him only three seconds, while the top-to-bottom took seven. He even used two shaving brushes to lather his face, because he found that by so doing he could cut seventeen seconds off his shaving time. For a while he tried shaving with two razors, but he finally gave that up.

"I can save forty-four seconds," he grumbled, "but I wasted two minutes this morning putting this bandage on my throat."

It wasn't the slashed throat that really bothered him. It was the two minutes.

Gilbreth and Gilbreth Carey (1972, pp. 2-3)

The man who pushed himself and his entire family in this way was Frank G. Gilbreth. The quotation above is taken from his biography. It is a remarkably affectionate account of the man, considering the fact that it is authored by two of his 12 children, Frank Gilbreth, Jr., and Ernestine Gilbreth Carey. Gilbreth was one of the pioneers of the school of rational work administration, often known as scientific management. This school of organization theory, through the use of job analyses and time-and-motion studies, attempts to establish normal times for various tasks within industrial production.[1] A colleague of Gilbreth's, Frederick W. Taylor (1911/1969), was responsible for the most authoritative formulation of these ideas in his book *The Principles of Scientific Management.*

The picture given above of the consequences of the struggle for efficiency in the home of the Gilbreth family should be supplemented with the view of how scientific management, or Taylorism, appeared when it was employed on a larger scale.

> [Taylor] looked upon the enterprise like a machine in which the different cogs and wheels were to have their specialized tasks. The worker by nature was lazy and only by supervision, stern discipline, and piece rate payment could [he] be persuaded to execute what was necessary for the functioning of the enterprise. . . . By dividing work into short cycles of just a few operations it was possible with the help of motion analysis, adjustment of the work places, and tools, to increase efficiency in manifold ways. By using the piece rate payment system, workers (who usually were not given any education) were made to carry out the monotonous work at a quick pace. It need hardly be said that the freedom of the worker in such a system was utterly restricted. The zenith (or perhaps rather the bottom level) of the development of Taylorism is the assembly line, where workers at predetermined pace repeatedly carry out a small number of operations. (Karlsson, 1969, pp. 56-57)

Monotony, the piece-rate system, and the strivings to make the worker an almost mechanical component of the machine, stand as monuments to alienation and routinization in industrial work. Since the 1930s organizational sociologists, social psychologists, and psychologists have tried to find solutions to, or rather compensatory arrangements for, those problems that are created by the extreme division of work, the piece-rate system, and time-and-motion studies.

The so-called human relations school (e.g., Mayo, 1933; Roethlisberger & Dickson, 1947; Walker & Guest, 1952) created somewhat of a sensation within organizational sociology with its discovery that shop-floor workers possessed the need for social contact and that formation of social groups was in response to this need. Gradually, it became more and more outdated to view the organization, or the industrial enterprise which was the most common object of study, like a machine that was rationally constructed and composed of parts that, if necessary, could be replaced by others. A systems perspective slowly emerged, i.e., a view of the organization as a living entity, striving for balance and equilibrium, continuously adjusting to forces within the system itself as well as to those in its surroundings.

The often inhuman consequences of Taylorism, the opposition by the human relations school, and the organization-theoretical systems approach, have been strong forces behind the currently common rejections of the rationalistic assumptions on which scientific management is based. Litterer (1969) portrays the association between rationalism and the classical school (Gilbreth, Taylor, Fayol, and others) in the following way:

> The classical point of view holds that work or tasks can be so organized as to accomplish efficiently the objectives of the organization. An organization is viewed as a product of rational thought concerned largely with coordinating tasks through the use of legitimate authority. It is based on the fundamental and usually implicit assumption that the behavior of people is logical, rational, and within the same system of rationality as that used to formulate the organization. (Vol. I, p. 6)

The basis of the rational theory of organizations has largely passed into oblivion, partly because of the attacks by other theoretical schools, and partly because it never actually received any authoritative scientific support. Gilbreth and Taylor were engineers primarily interested in exploiting their discoveries in practical manuals to increase the efficiency of industrial work. The "implicit assumption that the behavior of people is . . . rational" remained implicit, and was never developed into any explicit theory about organizations.

The classical school in organization sociology was normative in character. Because of this, it has been a favorite punching bag for organizational theoreticians within the human relations and systems traditions. These theoreticians claim to be more "scientific" in their approach, describing organizations "as they actually function" rather than how they would like them to function (see Chapter 6, "The Systems Perspective and Organizational Goals"). The practical consulting ambitions of the representatives of the scientific management school,[2] however, is not a sufficient reason, in and of itself, for rejecting the basic assumptions of the classical school in its effort to set up a goal-directed structure capable of carrying out work.

The following chapters deal with the description, discussion and critique of two main currents within organizational theory. Chapters 4, 5, and

6 contain presentations of the basic assumptions of the two traditions, rationalism and the systems perspective. Chapters 7 and 8 are devoted to a criticism and evaluation of the two perspectives. Both these outlooks have important weaknesses, but a review of the two would appear to favor the rationalistic one. In Chapter 9, I develop a process model for the study of organizations. This model draws on the some aspects of the rationalistic perspective, but at the same time tries to supplement it by making explicit references to the material and political conditions which constitute the frame factors or organizational behavior and restrict the organization's freedom to act. This discussion is summarized in Figure 9.1, and reference to this figure will facilitate the reading of Chapters 7 and 8. Chapters 10 and 11 are summaries that contain comments for later debate on organization theory.

The term *administration theory* used in that part of the book was chosen to emphasize that the following pages do not comprise a collection of rules or recipes for good organization (something that is fairly commonplace in books in this field). I have devoted relatively little space to the different varieties of the anatomy of organizations and the connection between a given administrative structure and, for example, production or administrative efficiency.

There are three reasons for this, in addition to the limitations of space. First, there are a large number of books available that target the consultant world: yet another examination of the advantages and disadvantages of, for example, line organization, function organization, product organization, project organization, matrix organization, etc. would not add much to the existing overabundance of good advice for administrators (Sjöstrand, 1987, gives a good exposition). Second, the choice of a suitable organization model is so strongly influenced by factors related to the situation and the surroundings that it is hardly possible to make any general recommendations. And third, most systems and rules may be reduced to a number of fairly simple principles for the grouping of activities in an organization (where, once again, the choice of principle is influenced by the situation: there is hardly a best solution for all circumstances). I refer the reader to Stewart's (1976) very systematic discussion of these principles.

Notes

1. The first MTM system was probably Gilbreth's invention *therbligs* (his name in reverse with slight variation): a series of standardized units of behavior like *search, find, select, take,* etc. The system was tested, for example, when Gilbreth had a doctor remove the tonsils of six of his children in one day, filming the operations (Gilbreth & Gilbreth Carey, 1972, chap. 10).

2. The principles for the administrative division of work, which were established by Gulick and Urwick (1937) in their *Papers on the Science of Administration,* are sometimes called administrative management. The differences between administrative management and scientific management is not great enough to require a special commentary.

4

Theoretical Outlooks:
Rationalism and the Systems Perspective

Introduction

In Part I of this book, I reviewed three different types of theories of bureaucracy. One of my conclusions was that Marxism lacks a theory about the inner structure of organizations and about the relationship between this structure and the efficiency of organizations. Marxism is first and foremost a theory about external conditions, i.e., material and structural-political conditions on which organizations are dependent. If we concern ourselves with a detailed analysis of organizations, Marxist theory (as it has traditionally been formulated) does not give us many useful starting points. With Weber and Michels, however, it is another matter. As we have seen, the theories of both of these authors contain large measures of "immanent" explanations of the actions of organizations. Also, the links backward to Weber and Michels in present-day organization theory are often very evident.

One may see Weber and Michels as representatives of two different and separate analytical schools concerned with the explanation of the inner structure and behavior of organizations. Weber represents a rationalistic, instrumentalistic approach. This is an approach in which the calculating and planning aspects of the actions of organizations are emphasized. Michels, on the other hand, exemplifies the systems perspective of organizations, according to which oligarchic phenomena emerge because of automatic processes of differentiation between the elite and the mass. Whereas Weber emphasizes prediction and plan, Michels emphasizes those aspects that are spontaneous and that arise "out of themselves." In this chapter, I shall briefly describe and comment on these two approaches to organization theory: rationalism and the systems perspective. A starting point for the discussion is a well-known article by Gouldner (1959), "Organizational Analysis."

Gouldner on Rationalism and Systems

The growth of large, complex organizations is one of the most distinctive characteristics of modern society and something that separates it from feudal societal forms. The French philosopher Saint-Simon was one of the first to pay attention to the emergence of modern patterns of organization. He identified some of their most characteristic traits. In the future, said Saint-Simon, administration would not be practiced by force or violence. The authority of the administrator would no longer be based on ascriptive characteristics, but rather, his authority would stem from his mastering of scientific and technical knowledge. With the rise of the modern professions (doctors, lawyers, engineers, etc.), occupational loyalties would emerge and extend outside the professional's own native and local community.

There exists, according to Gouldner, a clear parallel between Saint-Simon and Weber. Both emphasize the importance of expertise and scientific knowledge for the modern organization and its administration. In addition they both thoroughly spell out the ways in which the new organizations would affect the character of modern society. The primary difference between them is that Weber, more clearly than Saint-Simon, saw that authority in organizations was dependent not only on superior technical knowledge but also on factors of a less rational kind (e.g., charisma).

Another line of development connects Comte with modern systems theory. Gouldner notes one statement by Comte: "the final order which arises spontaneously is always superior to that which human combination had, by anticipation, constructed." In Comte's system, the "natural" and spontaneously achieved existing order is put forward instead of a political, legal, or constitutional order, which is planned. This idea of a natural system was later adopted and developed by Michels and even later by theoreticians within the structural-functional tradition, e.g., Parsons (Gouldner, 1959, p. 404). Gouldner describes the two approaches in the following way.

The Rational Model. The organization is viewed as an *instrument,* i.e., a rationally designed means for the realization of explicit goals of a particular group of people. The organizational structure is regarded as a tool, and alterations of the organizational structure are seen as instruments for improving efficiency.

> The rational model assumes that decisions are made on the basis of a rational survey of the situation, utilizing certified knowledge with a deliberate orientation to an expressly codified legal apparatus. The focus is, therefore, on the legally prescribed structure—ie., the formally "blueprinted" patterns—since these are more largely subject to deliberate inspection and rational manipulation. (Gouldner, 1959, pp. 404-405)

The rational model implies a *mechanical* perspective: "it views the organization as a structure of manipulable parts, each of which is separately modifiable with a view to enhancing the efficiency of the whole. Individual organizational elements are seen as subject to successful and planned modification, enactable by deliberate decision. The long-range development of the organization as a whole is also regarded as subject to planned control and as capable of being brought into increasing conformity with explicitly held plans and goals" (Gouldner, 1959, p. 405).

Thus modifications of the organization take place as the direct effects of the plans of a certain group (the mandator), with these modifications being made for the expressed purposes of implementing the mandator's plans. Changes are made in a deliberate manner, and the replacement or modifications of one part can be carried out without significantly affecting the other parts.

The Systems Perspective. Perhaps the most significant characteristic of a system is that changes in one part of it affect other parts as well. The different components of the system are dependent on each other. Changes are responses to the functional needs of the system or needs existing in the environment of the subsystem under study. According to the rational model, different parts of the organization may be changed without causing a disturbance in the other parts. According to the systems model, however, this is not possible since all parts are necessarily interdependent. Striving toward balance and survival are major characteristics of a natural system.

> The natural-system model regards the organization as a "natural whole," or system. The realization of the goals of the system as a whole is but one of several important needs to which the organization is oriented. Its component structures are seen as emergent institutions, which can be understood only in relation to the diverse needs of the total system. The organization, according to this model, strives to survive and to maintain its equilibrium, and this striving may persist even after its explicitly held goals have been successfully attained. This strain toward survival may even on occasion lead to the neglect or distortion of the organization's goals. Whatever the plans of their creators, organizations, say the natural-system theorists, become ends in themselves

and possess their own distinctive need which have to be satisfied. Once established, organizations tend to generate new ends which constrain subsequent decisions and limit the manner in which the nominal group goals can be pursued.

Organization structures are viewed as spontaneously and almost homeostatically maintained. Changes in organizational patterns are considered the results of cumulative, unplanned, adaptive responses to threats to the equilibrium of the system as a whole. Responses to problems are thought of as taking the form of crescively developed defense mechanisms and as being importantly shaped by shared values which are deeply internalized in the members. The empirical focus is thus directed to the spontaneously emergent and normatively sanctioned structures in the organization. . . .

The natural-system model is typically based upon an underlying "organismic" model which stresses the interdependence of the component parts. Planned changes are therefore expected to have ramifying consequences for the whole organizational system. . . . Long-range organizational development is . . . regarded as an evolution, conforming to "natural laws" rather than to the planner's designs. (Gouldner, 1959, pp. 405-406)

The distinction between rationalism and the systems perspective is of utmost importance within modern organizational theory. As we shall find, the two philosophical traditions are reflected in a great variety of theoretical contributions by well-known social science writers, some of whom are discussed in the following sections.

Open and Closed Systems:
Organizational Balance and Survival

Thompson (1967) has taken up Gouldner's (1959) distinction for further development. Thompson draws a parallel between, on the one hand, the rational model and the vision of a closed system, and on the other hand, what Gouldner calls the natural-systems model and the idea of an open system. As exponents of the *closed* tradition, he identifies Taylor and the scientific management school, Gulick and Urwick and their theory of administrative management, and Weber's model of bureaucracy (Thompson, 1967, pp. 4-6). Representatives of the *open* tradition are, e.g., Roethlisberger and Dickson, Barnard, Simon, and Selznick.

Thompson strongly stresses the character of the rational model as being a theory for planning and control of organizations. To his mind, it is primarily designed as a theory of efficiency and not as a theory of how organizations actually function.

It seems clear that the rational-model approach uses a closed-system strategy. . . . All resources are appropriate resources, and their allocation fits a
master plan. All action is appropriate action, and its outcomes are predictable.

It is no accident that much of the literature on the management or administration of complex organizations centers on the concepts of *planning* or
controlling. Nor is it any accident that such views are dismissed by those using
the open-system strategy. (Thompson, 1967, p. 6)

Concerning the open-systems model, Thompson directs our attention to
one feature that forms an important part of organizational systems theories: the assumption that the equilibrium of the system is maintained
through a balance between the contributions given by the participants of
the organization and the rewards received by them.

Approached as a natural system, the complex organization is a set of interdependent parts which together make up a whole because each contributes
something and receives something from the whole, which in turn is interdependent with some larger environment. Survival of the system is taken to
be the goal, and the parts and their relationships presumably are determined
through evolutionary processes. Dysfunctions are conceivable, but it is assumed that an offending part will adjust to produce a net positive contribution
or be disengaged, or else the system will degenerate. (Thompson, 1967,
pp. 6-7)

Rationalism and the Systems Perspective: Some Related Theories

The two perspectives stress different aspects of the inner structure of
organizations. In this section, I shall review some conceptual dichotomies
and distinctions presented by other authors that should be of particular
interest for our discussions here.

Burns and Stalker on Mechanistic and Organic Systems

Burns and Stalker (1961), in their book *The Management of Innovation,*
deal with the conditions for renewal and change in organizations. Their
major thesis is that the adequacy of a particular organizational structure is
contingent on the conditions under which the system works. They perceive
two opposite types of administrative systems, namely (1) the mechanistic
and (2) the organic.

The mechanistic system is best suited for stable conditions, i.e., when
the organization is not subject to many pressures toward change. The

organic form of organization, however, is more adequate when the environment of the organization is unstable and varying. For example, the organic form is better adapted to tasks that cannot be easily distributed between different positions in the organization. Thus the major formula is that a stable environment allows a rigid organizational structure, whereas a changing environment requires a structure which is loose and adaptable. The major traits of the mechanistic vis-à-vis the organic structural type are presented in the following sketch.

A *mechanistic system* is characterized by

a. The specialized differentiation of functional tasks into which the problems and tasks facing the concern as a whole are broken down.

b. The abstract nature of each individual task, which is pursued with techniques and purpose more or less distinct from those of the concern as a whole, i.e., the functionaries tend to pursue the technical improvement of means rather than the accomplishment of the ends of the concern.

c. The reconciliation, for each level in the hierarchy, of these distinct performances by the immediate superiors, who are also, in turn, responsible for seeing that each is relevant in his or her own special part of the main task.

d. The precise definition of rights and obligations and technical methods attached to each functional role.

e. The translation of rights, obligations, and methods into the responsibilities of a functional position.

f. Hierarchic structure of control, authority, and communication.

g. A reinforcement of the hierarchic structure by the location of knowledge of actualities exclusively at the top of the hierarchy, where the final reconciliation of distinct tasks and assessment of relevance is made.

h. A tendency for interaction between members of the concern to be vertical, i.e., between superior and subordinate.

i. A tendency for operations and working behavior to be governed by the instructions and decisions issued by superiors.

j. Insistence on loyalty to the concern and obedience to superiors as a condition of membership.

k. A greater importance and prestige attaching to internal (local) than to general (cosmopolitan) knowledge, experience, and skill.

An *organic system* is characterized by

a. The contributive nature of special knowledge and experience to the common task of the concern.

b. The "realistic" nature of the individual task, which is seen as set by the total situation of the concern.

c. The adjustment and continual redefinition of individual tasks through inter-action with others.

d. The shedding of "responsibility" as a limited field of rights, obligations and methods. Problems may not be posted upward, downward, or sideways as being someone else's responsibility.

e. The spread of commitment to the concern beyond any technical definition.

f. A network structure of control, authority, and communication.

g. Omniscience no longer imputed to the head of the concern; knowledge about the technical or commercial nature of the here-and-now task may be located anywhere in the network.

h. A lateral rather than a vertical direction of communication through the organization, communication between people of different rank, also resem-bling consultation rather than command.

i. A content of communication that consists of information and advice rather than instructions and decisions.

j. Commitment to the concern's tasks and to the "technological ethos" of material progress and expansion is more highly valued than loyalty and obedience.

k. Importance and prestige attached to affiliations and expertise valid in the industrial and commercial milieus external to the firm (Burns & Stalker, 1961, pp. 120-122).

The more "floating" character of the organic form does not mean that the organization is completely unstratified. The actors have a more or less valued position. Their performance, however, is evaluated primarily on the basis of demonstrated expert knowledge. The more experienced people will often assume leadership, but it is a fundamental assumption of an organic system that the one who is best informed and has the most relevant knowledge should become the leader.

The characteristic of the organic type of being a somewhat more open system is demonstrated by items j and k, which stress that the loyalties of the positions extend further than is the case in a mechanistic system. The organic model is also based more on mutual relationships, consultation, and continuous inner change. Participants are governed more by referring to long-range programs and aims rather than through detailed instructions or strict adherence to their contractual relationship with the organization. A relative absence of hierarchy, division of tasks, centralized information, and strict definitions of positions differentiate the organic model from the mechanistic.

Demonstration cases of the two organizational models are not difficult to find. The military organization or the assembly line car factory exem-plify the mechanistic variant; a scientific institution, a research depart-ment of a company, or a public relations office exemplify the organic.

Burns and Stalker (1961) emphasize that their conceptual dichotomy is not only a theoretical construction. The concepts are not "merely interpretations offered by observers of different schools," but are forms of organization that "exist objectively" (p. 119). This approach can be contrasted to Gouldner's (1959), which contends that the rationalist type of theory and the systems perspective represent different *theoretical ideal* types (pp. 406-407).

The issue about different *empirical structures* of the organization should not be mixed with the question of advantages of drawbacks of particular *organizational theories*. Burns and Stalker's approach implies that the two types of structural models are more or less suitable solutions to particular organizational problems, with the choice between a mechanistic and organic solution, depending on environmental conditions. In contrast to the distinction between mechanistic and organic structures, the rationalist perspective and the systems perspective represent theoretical points of departure for observing the organization as a totality. This total perspective includes, but is not the same as, the views of what is an adequate (or inadequate) inner structure in a particular situation.

Argyris, Likert, Perrow, and Others

Conceptions about the latent conflict between a mechanistic structure and a humanistic development—an optimistic and dealienating view of man—are very common in the organizational-sociological literature. For example, Argyris states that there exists a contradiction between properties of the individual and certain organizational characteristics. According to him the development of the individual is characterized by an increasing motivation to take initiatives, to learn and develop, to take on still greater responsibility, and to make more and more encompassing decisions. When the individual is fit into a mechanistic organization, however, he becomes the object of pressures in the opposite direction, i.e., pressures to subordinate himself, to carry out routine and monotonous tasks, to take on very limited responsibility, and to make few, if any, important decisions (Argyris, 1967). Thus a major line of thought in Argyris's (1964) work is that the organic type of organization should be sought after when "decisions in which maximum individual productivity and maximum feelings of responsibility and commitment are desired—for example, decisions regarding promotion, salaries, or the acceptance of a departmental production objective" (p. 210). In other words, the organic type of organization is better able to produce harmony between individual characteristics and organizational demands. Within the organic type of organization, which is made up of "essential properties," the individual has greater possibilities of achieving "positive mental health" (Argyris, 1964, pp. 160ff.). (*Essential properties* means, briefly, that the organization approaches organic characteristics, i.e., develops interrelations between different parts, achieves goals that are related to the whole system rather than parts of the system, and maintains balance and equilibrium (pp. 119ff.).

Likert (1961), in his book *New Patterns of Management,* distinguishes an authoritarian form of organization from one where the individual participates and cooperates. Authoritarian organizational forms can vary from being directly exploitive to benignly authoritarian. In the participate forms, decisions are made by the total organization. The authoritarian form is characterized by one-sided control, whereas the participative one has a more collectively distributed control (Likert, 1961, pp. 423ff.).

Other authors who present dichotomous pictures of organization via the use of concepts that emphasize rigid as opposed to loose structures (or closed versus open structure) are McGregor (1960), Bennis (1959), Barnes (1960), and Litwak (1961). For example, McGregor contrasts an open and more philanthropic theory of management (*theory Y*) to a theory that is more closed and authoritarian (*theory X*). Bennis describes the organic organization as problem solving. Barnes uses the concept of open system, and Litwak bases his discussion on the term *human relations.*

Of particular interest in this connection is an article by Perrow (1967). Perrow suggests that organizations should be classified in regard to what type of technology they use and by what types of decisions are required by production. According to Perrow, it is especially important to distinguish organizations with routine production from those with nonroutine production. In routine production, the organization encounters few situations that present unusual or abnormal demands; it has to master few exceptional cases or particular circumstances, and it can draw on well-established, standardized logical and analytical methods for solving problems. In nonroutine production, the situation is the reverse. The organization encounters a multitude of previously unknown problems and does not have recourse to established problem-solving routines. A good example of the latter case is the space industry and, of the former, steel production (Perrow, 1967, pp. 195-196). A more mechanistic structure is to be expected in steel production than in the space industry.

5

Rationalism and Means-Ends Analysis

Introduction

In the previous chapter, I outlined certain traits that separate the rational-istic perspective of organizations from the systems perspective. In addition, I pointed out how the differentiation of a rationalism and systems perspective is related to a variety of other well-known organizational-theoretical approaches. In this chapter, I shall go further into the basic assumptions of the rationalist theory and provide some examples of rationalistic analysis.

The rationalist approach has two basic characteristics. First, the actions of organizations are seen as a *function of goals,* which are set up by some individual or group of individuals (the organization's mandator). Second, it is assumed that the person or persons who are able to implement the goals on a day-to-day basis are capable of carrying out an *inventory of different alternative ways of reaching the organization goals* and that the individual is able to choose an adequate means for performing the chosen strategy in the most economical fashion.

The Anatomy of the Decision Process

Goal Rationality and Value Rationality

Social action, according to Weber (1968, p. 24) is goal rational or instrumentally rational (*zweckrational*) when it is based on the expectation of the actions of other people and objects in the environment. The actor uses these expectations as conditions or means to achieve his or her own con-sciously pursued goals. According to the model of goal-rational behavior, the individual strives to evaluate in one composite calculus the goals, means, and possible secondary consequences of his or her action. This means that the individual consciously and deliberately surveys alternative ways of reaching his or her goal, that the individual relates the goal to the secondary consequences, and that the individual tries to estimate the relative importance of different possible goals (Weber, 1968, p. 26). Goal-rational behavior differs from value-rational (*wertrational*) action, the latter is determined by "a conscious belief in the value for its own sake of some ethical, aesthetic, religious, or other form of behavior, *independently* of its prospects of success" (Weber, 1968, pp. 24-25; emphasis added).

The bureaucratic ideal type, sketched out by Weber and subject to much sociological controversy, can be seen as a survey of the organizational and administrative arrangements that are best suited to achieve full goal rationality in organized action (see box in Chapter 2). The bureaucratic ideal type is a theoretical construction, a kind of measuring device against which one can compare different empirical cases.

There is a multitude of misunderstandings associated with the bureaucratic ideal type. In U.S. organizational sociology, considerable effort has been devoted to the task of showing or implying that the bureaucratic organization is not optimally effective. The most well known analysis of this kind is Merton's (1957) article "Bureaucratic Structure and Personality." A similar thesis is advanced by Michel Crozier (1964) in *The Bureaucratic Phenomenon*. Merton points out, among other things, that the official in an administrative system often develops a behavior in which discipline becomes an immediate value, with the original goals of the organization tending to be displaced and subordinated to his or her loyalty to rules ("an instrumental value becomes a terminal value," Merton, 1957, p. 199). Furthermore, the official, because of his or her concentration on special areas of competence, may develop what Veblen calls "trained incapacity," i.e., a condition in which the official's expert knowledge functions as an obstacle to flexibility and creativity.

In his description of the bureaucratic type of organization, Merton (1952) emphasizes the dysfunctions of bureaucracy, in contrast to the positive aspects brought forward by Weber, or rather, the positive aspects that Weber seems to have brought forward. Merton presents the bureaucratic ideal type as if Weber had given it only positive connotations. According to Merton (1957), Weber's analysis implies that "the positive attainments and functions of bureaucratic organization are emphasized and the internal stresses and strains of such structures are almost wholly neglected" (p. 197). In a similar way, Crozier (1964, pp. 187ff.) emphasizes that a bureaucratic organization has several negative effects, the significant characteristic of bureaucracy being a tendency toward inability to adjust adequately to changes in the environment of the organization.

The contributions of Merton and Crozier are excellent pieces of sociological analysis and contain many important arguments. However, I find it difficult to see them as valid criticisms of Weber. Weber did not maintain that the bureaucratic organization necessarily is effective because of hierarchy, distribution of labor, universalism, etc., but, and this is an important distinction, that an organization with these characteristics is *capable* of reaching maximum possible efficiency (Weber, 1968, p. 223). This capacity of the bureaucratic form of organization is associated with its technical characteristics, and in these technical characteristics it is, according to Weber (1968, p. 223), superior to any other form of organization. As I have tried to show in the first part of this book, Weber emphasizes in many places the need for bureaucracy to be subordinate to its master. The list of German words that were used to characterize the Weberian ideal type in Chapter 1 (*Präzision, Schnelligkeit, Eindeutigkeit,* etc.) also included the important term *straffe Unterordnung* (strict subordination). The views advanced in part I of this book imply that the technical efficiency of the bureaucratic ideal type needs to be related to the purposes and goals that the organization is set up to accomplish. Thus, in certain respects, it seems pointless for Merton to object to Weber on the basis that the bureaucratic form of organization has certain dysfunctions that show themselves empirically as tendencies toward rigidity, displacement of goals, etc. As I have pointed out, Weber himself stressed these tendencies of the bureaucratic apparatus (note, for example, his analysis of Prussia after Bismarck), and he conceived of such characteristics precisely as dysfunctions, as deviations from the ideal type sketched by him (cf. Lindskoug, 1979).

The Elements of Rational Decision Making

Simon (1947/1957), in *Administrative Behavior,* developed a theory about the decision process in administrative systems. The book contains a detailed treatment of the anatomy of rational decision making, a discussion that takes place within a more general organizational-sociological framework of a systems character. One might say that Simon has separated from Weber's treatment of the bureaucratic form of organization that special part that deals with the logic of rational decision making. The historical aspects of goal-rational behavior are totally missing in Simon's book, which concentrates, rather, on the technicalities in the process of establishing goals and subgoals and choosing adequate means of action.

What is a decision? A complex decision (and the decision processes of organizations are complex) "is like a great river, drawing from its many tributaries the innumerable component premises of which it is constituted" (Simon, 1947/1957, p. xii). Many individuals and units of organization contribute to every decision. These contributions may be viewed as the preconditions for the final composite decision ("the river"), and therefore, according to Simon, it becomes meaningless to put the question, "Who really makes the decision?" (p. xii).

Organizational decision making is a kind of compromise between rational, goal-oriented behavior and nonrational action. Simon (1947/1957) suggests that a central field of administrative theory is "the boundary between the rational and the nonrational aspects of human social behavior" (p. xxiv). An organization, in Simon's perspective, is a structure that provides the framework for the decisions. The organization supplies every member of the group with the information, preconditions, and goals on which to base his or her decisions. In addition, it defines the space of action for other people in the organization to whom the decision maker has to relate.

The conflict between the rational and the nonrational in human behavior means that administrative theory has to take into account the fact that the behavior of human beings can never be at an optimum. According to Simon, people act in order to achieve satisfying solutions, since they do not have the ability to reach the best solutions by absolute standards. "While economic man maximizes—selects the best alternatives from among all those available to him, his cousin, whom we shall call administrative man, satisfices—looks for a course of action that is satisfactory or 'good enough' " (Simon, 1947/1957, p. xxiv).

> An alternative is *optimal* if: (1) there exists a set of criteria that permits all alternatives to be compared, and (2) the alternative in question is preferred by these criteria, to all other alternatives. An alternative is *satisfactory* if: (1) there exists a set of criteria that describes minimally satisfactory alternatives, and (2) the alternative in question meets or exceeds all these criteria. (March & Simon, 1958, p. 140)

Note the extremely strong demands that are put on the decision-making process in the optimum case. In principle, all known alternatives should be possible to compare, after which the best alternative is chosen. In the case of satisfying solutions, it is enough that some alternative corresponding to certain minimum criteria is chosen. The difference between the two ways of action may be illustrated with the situation of searching through a haystack to find the *most sharp-pointed* needle hidden in the haystack, in comparison with the situation of finding a needle that is *sharp-pointed enough* (Simon, 1947/1957, p. 141).

Let us look closer at the meaning of Simon's concept of decision process. A decision process may be defined as a choice among alternatives that are perceived as adequate means for achieving pursued goals. These goals, however, in themselves are means for reaching more final purposes, or ultimate goals. On ultimate goals, see Langefors (1970). The term refers to the ultimate aims of the organization, or "the reason that the activity, or the system, is kept running." Below the ultimate goals are goals of lower priority. These subgoals should ideally be consistent with the ultimate goals. "Thus, one has to have some conception of which ultimate goals one wants to pursue in order to judge the efficiency of the subgoals, this being necessary also in order to allow for estimations of total efficiency" (Langefors, 1970, p. 22).

Goals are founded on *values*. Simon (1947/1957, pp. 45-46) explicitly accepts logical empiricism and its emphasis on the distinction between propositions of fact and propositions of value. Propositions of fact can be tested by empirical observation, whereas propositions of value have "imperative quality," i.e., they select a certain future condition at the cost of one or several others. Because decisions contain value as well as factual statements, they cannot be objectively described as correct or incorrect.

The decision process has to start with some value premise that is taken as given. According to Simon (1947/1957, p. 50), this "ethical premise" is represented in organizations by the description of organizational objectives. The objective has to be described in such concrete terms that it is possible to determine to what degree the goals have been implemented as a result of organizational action.

To achieve a certain goal, one will usually employ a variety of different strategies. The achievement of a goal, therefore, demands a choice between alternative strategies. In the evaluation of strategies, all those consequences that follow from each alternative should be judged. *Consequences,* according to this optimum model, is a term comprising not only those outcomes that were predicted from the beginning but also those effects that were not originally predicted.

After establishing the goal, the decision may be described as a process of four steps: (1) Make an inventory of all alternative strategies (A_i), (2) establish which consequences (c_{ij}) will follow from every A_i, (3) carry out evaluations (V_{ij}) of the consequences taking into account the established goals, and (4) choose a strategy (i.e., make a decision) (Simon, 1947/1957, p. 67).

The "decision tree" (Figure 5.1) illustrates the process.

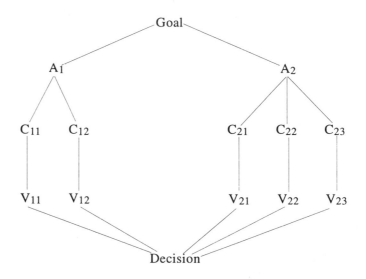

Figure 5.1. The Decision Tree

NOTE: For similar models of the decision process, see, for example, Hedberg, Sjöberg & Targama (1971, p. 63) and Rhenman (1968, p. 43).

Applications of Means-Ends Theory

In his book *Sweden: Prototype of Modern Society,* Tomasson (1970) writes:

> Swedes believe that institutions can and should be restructured to accomplish certain agreed-upon ends. This is true in spite of the fact that the traditional component in many Swedish institutions is great, particularly in the government, the universities, and the legal system. . . . Contemporary Sweden abounds in examples of change in the most fundamental institutions. . . . The radical restructuring of the school system to make it more egalitarian is one example. The radical revision of the constitution to bring it in accord with contemporary practice is another example. . . . Even sex roles and the relations between the sexes are believed to be amenable to change through changing educational and economic institutions. (pp. 274-275)

The times have changed, and so has Swedish society. The optimistic picture painted by Tomasson in 1970 has lost some color, and the policy for greater equality did not become quite the success he expected. But Tomasson is quite right in his judgment on the ambitions of the Swedish reform policy. The emphasis on empiricism and rationality, which Tomasson sees as dominant values in Swedish society, is well exhibited by the Swedish parliamentary reports (*Statens Offentliga Utredningar,* or *SOU*). Partly because they recruit members from a broad spectrum of political parties at an early stage in their work, the parliamentary committees tend to emphasize compromise rather than ideological conflict. This is also due to the fact that the committees are anxious to seek the cooperation of experts from different fields and of different persuasions to ensure maximum objectivity. Their reports, therefore, "tend to be factual, filled with statistics, and parsimonious in the use of generalizations and assumptions." (Tomasson, 1970, p. 274). This becomes especially clear if the Swedish reports are compared with the British government reports. "The Swedish reports take little for granted, whereas the British reports are replete with ideological assumptions and general beliefs" (p. 274).

The example of a classical Swedish parliamentary report, given below, well illustrates the "secular rationalism" and the "instrumental attitude toward institutions" that Tomasson has found to be characteristic of Swedish society. It illustrates how the rational approach is employed for overseeing procedures in social welfare and social work. The many evaluations of social, educational, and labor market reforms that have taken place during the 1970s and 1980s in Sweden often use the approach illustrated below (cf. Nilstun, 1980).

The Survey of Social Legislation, 1974

The social legislation survey states that the formulation of precise goals is a precondition for decision making regarding social service organizations, for the relation of social services to other societal areas, and for the cooperation between the social service authorities and other organizations. In addition, explicit goals are needed for the development of working methods, the legislative specification of social service tasks, etc. and, most important, to ensure that social service activity can be made subject to follow-ups and evaluation of results (*SOU,* 1974, pp. 39, 157ff.).

The goals, therefore, become both the starting point and the end point of the activities within social care, social treatment, and social planning. The scheme of principles for the solution of social problems, sketched out by the committee, is also designed to function as a guideline for the individual social worker and for his or her way of making decisions when confronted with the various problems. The committee argues that the sketch for the solution of social problems (shown in Figure 5.2) is applicable to all three areas of social service, namely (1) individual and family

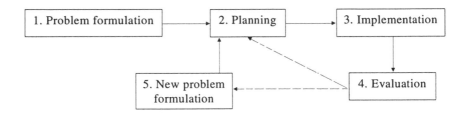

Figure 5.2. The Sketch for the Solution of Social Problems

SOURCE: *SOU* (1974, pp. 39, 356).

treatment, (2) community work, and (3) social planning (*SOU,* 1974, pp. 39, 355-356).

Figure 5.2 contains five steps and starts with a social worker together with a client trying to describe the current situation for the client, in order to see what problems it may contain (problem formulation). One tries to answer the questions Which causes lie behind the client's present situation? To what extent can the client himself or herself affect this situation?

The second step (planning) is the formulation of goals, analysis of action alternatives and evaluation of the effects and causes of these alternatives. In regard to goals, the committee states that the general goals that have been indicated and commented on in the committee report (i.e., democracy, equality, and security) should function as *targets* for the social worker (*SOU,* 1974, pp. 39, 357). For natural reasons, it is difficult to see how these goals are to be implemented in each specific case. Treatment, therefore, often has to be aimed at more short-sighted goals, or *subtargets.* After the goals have been established, the action alternatives are clarified. In this stage, the social worker tries to answer the question regarding which social services can be beneficially utilized in the case under consideration. Finally, within this step, the action alternatives are evaluated. Attempts are made to determine what effects the implemented actions may have on the client's situation and what are the costs of each alternative action. "It is . . . important that all costs are taken into consideration. . . . On the other hand, it cannot be required that every social worker make a complete review of resource assets and costs" (*SOU,* 1974, p. 357).

Before leaving box 2 in Figure 5.2, a decision should have been made, by comparing the expected effects of each action alternative with the resources required to implement it. It may then happen that

> none of [the action alternatives] offers a satisfactory solution with regard to the established goal, or that the costs of achieving the goal appear too high. If so, the

goal should be re-evaluated. With regard to a new goal, one performs a new analysis of the available action alternatives, etc. (*SOU,* 1974, pp. 39, 357)

Once a plan for treatment has been worked out, we then enter the third step of the means-end scheme and carry out the action program decided on. Assuming that the action program can be performed without too many problems (if not, the program should be modified), we can then move to the fourth step, i.e., the evaluation of the performed work. This evaluation should contain the following:

First, continuous documentation of the actions taken and the changes which are achieved in the life conditions of the client or the group . . . and of the results which have been achieved in relationship to the established goals. Second, an analysis with the purpose of providing a basis for possible modifications of social service operations. (*SOU,* 1974, pp. 39, 358)

It is hoped that this evaluation process will provide experience such that a new problem area can be formulated, and thereafter, the process starts anew from box 2, with new planning, implementation, etc.

6

The Systems Perspective:
Some Basic Characteristics

Systems Theory and
Structural-Functionalism

Looking at organizational theory today, we find it surprisingly unaffected by the sometimes violent critical discussions about the functionalist school that have been going on in sociology for the last 20 years. The systems perspective, which takes many of its essential traits from functionalism, has strongly dominated organizational sociology and has developed under the influence of writers such as Chester I. Barnard, Herbert A. Simon, James G. March, D. Katz and R. L. Kahn, and Amitai Etzioni.

Structural-functionalism emphasizes the idea that society has a stable character and is made up of a well-integrated structure of elements. To the structural-functionalist, the *structure* of the social system is founded on a consensus between the members on values and norms, and furthermore, the different elements of society fulfill *functions* that contribute to the maintenance of the system. The system's survival, its equilibrium, and the balanced relationship between its various parts are three essential components of both functionalist sociological theory and the systems variant of organizational sociology. Two Norwegian organizational researchers, H. M. Blegen and B. Nyléhn (1969), say in the introduction of their book *Organisasjonsteori:*

> When we study organizations, it is fruitful to look upon the world as composed of systems. The systems theory, which we take as our point of departure, is still not a unified discipline. It represents today a very incomplete construction which can be only partially described, and at that, only in an imprecise and

qualitative way. Still, the *idea* which is the basis of this theory is acknowledged by scientists from a large variety of professional fields, a model of the world where everything is contingent upon everything—"wheels within wheels within wheels"—where the mutual relations and the reciprocal communication between systems, subsystems, and superordinate systems are the fundamental characteristics. (p. 6)

The limitations of space do not allow a treatment of general systems theory as presented by Wiener, von Bertalanffy, Ashby, and others. Good introductory discussions on general systems theory may be found in Hall and Hagen (1956); and Emery (1969). I will limit myself to a few comments on the functionalist tradition within sociology, comments that are of importance for the discussion to follow.

Within sociology, functionalist ideas have had their most prominent spokesman in Parsons. The social system is described by Parsons as a number of individuals in mutual interrelationships with one another. Individuals cooperate because of their common motivation to achieve *optimum need gratification*. Their expectation is that their interaction with other individuals within the system carries greater need gratification for them than would result from their own individual activity or their activity in other systems. Thus the basis for their participation in the system is their expectation that a positive individual exchange balance will result (Parsons, 1951, pp. 5-6, chaps. 2, 3).

The notion of a positive balance of exchange as lying behind the motivation of individuals to participate in the organization (which, in its turn, is a precondition for the continued existence of the system) is a cornerstone in the theories of, among others, Simon (1947/1957), March and Simon (1958), Ramström (1964), and Rhenman (several works, see e.g., 1968); also see Chapter 8, "The Inducement-Contribution Balance" and the quotation from Thompson in Chapter 4, "Open and Closed Systems." As I will argue more specifically below, the idea of exchange balance also represents one of the major problems of the systems theory tradition in organizational sociology.

The fundamental mechanism for the integration and stabilization of social systems is *institutionalization*. Institutional patterns are patterns of expectations of *culturally adequate behavior,* expectations directed toward the role occupants of the system. Briefly, institutionalization is that process by which the adequate behavior of each individual in the system is insured, i.e., the process by which a certain way of acting becomes accepted by them as a positive value. The result of effective institutionalization is that each individual will accept the priority of collective interests over his or her own particularistic interests.

On Stakeholders

A key concept within the systems theory variant of organizational sociology is that of the *stakeholder* (*intressent,* or "participant" in March & Simon, 1958, pp. 89-90). The organization is perceived as a kind of market for various groups of stakeholders, i.e., different parties that find that they may have something to win by cooperating with the organization. In turn, the equilibrium of the organization is dependent on an undisturbed relationship between the organization and its different stakeholders. The organization as a system is contingent on this exchange with its environment; the character of the exchange varies with the different needs of the organization, and consequently, the set of stakeholders also differs from time to time and between organizations. Therefore, definition of a stakeholder must necessarily be somewhat arbitrary. The most important stakeholders in a commercial organization are the employees, investors, suppliers, distributors, and consumers (March & Simon, 1958, p. 89).

The pluralistic image of stakeholders or "participants," which has been developed within the systems theory tradition primarily by March and Simon, has become widely popular in Sweden, e.g., through the work of Eric Rhenman. Some of the organizational theorists who explicitly adopt the picture of the organization by Rhenman, following March and Simon, are Ramström (1964, p. 23), Mabon (1973, pp. 64ff.), Norrbom (1971, p. 78), Asplund (1973, p. 104), and Hedberg et al. (1971, p. 13). The stakeholders of the organization are those individuals or groups who are dependent on the enterprise for the implementation of their own personal needs and on whom the enterprise is dependent for its continued existence.

In contrast to the basic ideas of the rationalistic tradition, the systems perspective does not see the organization primarily as an instrument for the realization of the mandator's goals. Rather, the organization is perceived as a structure that responds to, and adjusts itself to, a multitude of demands from various stakeholders and that tries to maintain balance by reconciling these demands. The organization's management acquires a kind of mediator role, i.e., a role of weighing the demands from different stakeholders against each other. One can contrast this role description to that forwarded by the rationalistic tradition, in which the organizational management is seen more as the "extended arm" of the mandator.

The image of a set of stakeholders and the other primary components of the systems view of organizations, i.e., requirements for the system's survival and the balance between rewards and contributions, clearly emerges from the short and concise summary made by Simon (1947/1957) in the chapter "The Organizational Balance" from his book *Administrative Behavior:*

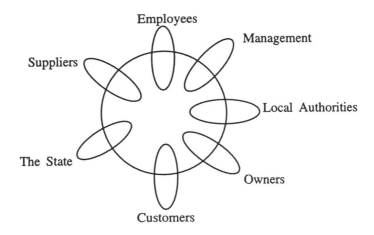

Figure 6.1. Stakeholders

SOURCE: Rhenman (1968, p. 25).

> The organization has been described in this chapter as a system in equilibrium, which receives contributions in the form of money or effort, and offers inducements in return for these contributions. These inducements include the organizational goal itself, conservation and growth of the organization, and incentives unrelated to these two.
>
> The organization equilibrium is maintained by the control group, whose personal values may be of various kinds, but who assume the responsibility of maintaining the life of the organization in order that they may attain these values. (p. 122)

To a large extent, Simon speaks here as an apostle of Barnard, whose book *The Functions of the Executive,* which appeared at the end of the 1930s, is perhaps the first comprehensive employment of systems theory for the purpose of enterprise government. Barnard (1968), for example, states the following: "The survival of an organization depends upon the maintenance of an equilibrium of complex character in a continuously fluctuating environment of physical, biological, and social materials, elements, and forces, which calls for readjustment of processes internal to the organization" (p. 6). Simon's systems perspective of the organization as a structure that directs and regulates individual decisions for the benefit of the totality is fully developed in Barnard's work as well. According to Barnard (1968, p. 14), the organization establishes limits to the individual's freedom of choice. Furthermore, Simon's discussion on the reward/contribution balance has a direct forerunner in

Barnard's (1968, pp. 140, 153) discussion. (For some further comments on the similarities between Barnard and Simon, see Krupp, 1961, pp. 91ff.).

Balance and Exchange

The criteria of balance and exchange are formulated by March and Simon (1958) in their very influential book *Organizations* in the following way:

> (1) An organization is a system of interrelated social behaviors of a number of persons whom we shall call the *participants* in the organization.
>
> (2) Each participant and each group of participants receives *from* the organization *inducements* in return for which he makes *to* the organization *contributions*.
>
> (3) Each participant will continue his participation in an organization only so long as the inducements offered him are as great or greater (measured in terms of *his* values and in terms of the alternatives open to him) than the contributions he is asked to make.
>
> (4) The contributions provided by the various groups of participants are the source from which the organization manufactures the inducements offered to participants.
>
> (5) Hence, an organization is "solvent"—and will continue in existence—only so long as the contributions are sufficient to provide inducements in large enough measure to draw forth these contributions. (p. 84)

Thus "equilibrium because of a positive balance of exchange for the participants" can be viewed as the basic summary thesis of the systems perspective within organizational sociology. Or, as Emery and Trist (1969) say in a much-quoted article titled "Sociotechnical Systems": "The continued existence of any enterprise presupposes some regular commerce in products or services with other enterprises, institutions and persons in its external social environment. If it is going to be useful to speak of steady states in an enterprise, they must be states in which this commerce is going on" (pp. 282-283).

Institutionalization

Institutionalization is a key concept within both functionalism and systems theory. The term refers to those processes and methods by which the organization inculcates a set of strategic values in the individuals who work in the organization. But how, more specifically, does the organization create consent around these values? This issue has been discussed by Selznick (1957) who argues for the importance of leadership for creating value homogeneity within the organization.

According to Selznick (1957), institutionalization means "to *infuse with value* beyond the technical requirements of the task at hand. . . . From the standpoint of the committed person, the organization is changed from an expendable tool into a valued source of personal satisfaction" (p. 17). Selznick emphasizes the importance of developing an administrative ideology, an official philosophy that is helpful in establishing a homogeneous staff in the organization and in guaranteeing continuity in the work of the leading group. "A well-formulated doctrine is remarkably handy for boosting internal morale, communicating the bases for decisions, and rebuffing outside claims and criticisms" (Selznick, 1957, p. 14).

Second, Selznick speaks of the importance of controlling the *creation and defense of elites*. It is a practical problem of great importance for organizations to form elite groups.

> Specialized academies, selective recruiting, and many other devices help to build up the self-consciousness and the confidence of present and potential leaders. However, . . . counter-pressures work to break down the insulation of these elites and to warp their self-confidence. A problem of institutional leadership, as of statesmanship generally, is to see that elites do exist and function while inhibiting their tendency to become sealed off and to be more concerned with their own fate than with that of the enterprise as a whole. (Selznick, 1957, p. 14)

The importance of uniform values in the organic type of organization can hardly get a more eloquent spokesman than Selznick: "The art of the creative leader is the art of institution-building, the reworking of human and technological materials to fashion an organism that embodies new and enduring values" (1957: 152-153).

It is not goal rationality, but rather, value rationality that dominates Selznick's description of the organization. One could say that Selznick's perspective on organizations, in contrast to Weber's, emphasizes the organization as an ideological and normative habitat for the individual. In such a perspective, the charismatic and policy-directed characteristics of leadership are made to dominate over the instrumental aspects, with the final result being a kind of manual for managers eager to build empires and institutions around a set of values that they consider necessary to promote and to conserve.

The Systems Perspective and Organizational Goals

The conception of an organization as a system, existing to fulfill the needs of certain stakeholders and constantly adjusting to environmental pressures and forces within the system itself, itself skeptical of any analysis of organizations in terms of goals. One of the most influential theoretical books on organizations appearing in the 1960s, Katz and Kahn's (1966) *The Social Psychology of Organizations,* strongly attacks the rationalistic approach and argues for the superiority of systems theory in the study of organizations. According to Katz and Kahn, the goals that have been laid down by the founders or initiators of the organization, as well as the goals that are regarded as important to the present leaders of the organization, cannot be used as the basis for a theory of organizations. The authors do accept that it would be wrong to discount the goals that organizations have deliberately built into the "social contracts" on which they are formed. However, and this is their main theme, such goals are often deceptive. Goal descriptions may idealize, explain away, hide, or even leave out certain essential aspects of organizational behavior. Which, then, are these essential aspects? The following quotation from Katz and Kahn (1966) shows where they think the answer can be found.

> The organization as a system has an output, a product or an outcome, but this is not necessarily identical with the individual purposes of group members. Though the founders of the organization and its key members do think in teleological terms about organizational objectives, we should not accept such practical thinking, useful as it may be, in place of a theoretical set of constructs for purposes of scientific analysis. Social science, too frequently in the past, has been misled by such short-cuts and has equated popular phenomenology with scientific explanation. (pp. 15-16)

Thus the systems-theoretical approach fulfills the requirements of being scientific, whereas rationalism does not. Assumptions concerning organizational goals "scarcely provide an adequate basis for the study of organizations and at times can be misleading and even fallacious" (Katz & Kahn, 1966, p. 14). According to the opinion of Katz and Kahn, systems theory in these respects differs favorably from what they call "common sense approaches" (p. 14).

Not all authors within the systems tradition are as critical of "common sense approaches" as Katz and Kahn, but I believe it is fair to say that systems theories are strongly ambivalent when confronted by the concept of goals or objectives. True, they often acknowledge that it is possible to distinguish a multitude of different goals within an organization. This acknowledgment, however, is usually accompanied by a denial that the organization has a superordinate or dominating goal. At the most, *goals* are treated as things that are associated with the various components of the organization (individuals, offices, departments, etc.), and quite often, there is a noted reluctance toward the idea that the leadership of an organization or a company may have more dominating goals than other groups within the organization. The systems-theoretical school emphasizes that even though goals may exist within the organization, the *action* of the organization need not be directly related to these goals. The difference between the rationalistic school and the systems perspective may best be explained in the following manner: In rationalistic theory, goals represent an independent variable and the organizational structure, a dependent variable. In the systems-theoretical school, both goals and structure are responses to functional needs within the organization and in the surrounding supersystem and, because of this, are dependent variables. The latter position implies that a good explanation or prediction of organizational behavior cannot be achieved as a result of research that primarily focuses on the organization's goals. Let us look somewhat closer into this problem.

Etzioni (1964, p. 5) stresses that goals supply orientations for organizations. They depict a future condition, lay down directions for organizational activity, represent a source of legitimacy, and function as a model against which one may gauge the efficiency of the organization. Almost all organizations have a formal body for setting goals and for reformulating them (p. 7). Etzioni (1964) also admits that organizations usually have some stakeholder or power group that has the ultimate command of the organization (pp. 10, 12).

As Etzioni (1964) argues, these factors, however, are not an adequate basis for a scientific study of organizations. It is true, he says, that organizations have goals. However, they also have needs that arise from their day-to-day activities and thus are tempted to satisfy their current needs at the cost of the original goals. Organizations often abandon their initial goals. Sometimes they also replace their primary goals with other goals, a process frequently associated with a bid for power by various professional groups (Etzioni, 1964, pp. 5, 9-12). Thus, during their daily operations, new goals and purposes arise that often clash with the original goals. (The discussion has a parallel in Perrow's, 1967, distinction between official and operative goals, see Chapter 9, "Official and Operative Goals.")

Etzioni (1964) puts forward another objection to the study of organizational goals. He argues that such studies can easily achieve the character of *social criticism* and in the process become less scientific. Because organizations rarely reach their goals, they can be too easily construed as inefficient. Therefore, organizations should not be compared with their ideals as formulated in their goals but with each other (pp. 16-17). (Etzioni overlooks the fact that organizations often have goals below the ideal or ultimate level, goals that are considerably more concrete and specific and that, better than the ultimate goals, may be used for a survey of organizational effectiveness; see Chapter 7.)

Etzioni (1964) finds the systems model more satisfactory to the scientific study of organizations. The systems perspective deals with the specification of those relations that have to exist in the organization in order for it to operate effectively (p. 17). Effectiveness involves the achievement not only of goals but also of so-called nongoal activities, an example is increasing employee motivation.

A similar viewpoint is put forward by Silverman (1970). He emphasizes that the possible advantage of classifying organizations in terms of goals is that the concept of goal offers a point of reference against which one may judge the system's "health" (p. 9). The problem, however, is that an organization can rarely be characterized as having any goal, thus rendering this approach as generally unfeasible. According to Silverman (1970), it is legitimate to conceive of an organization as having a goal only in the case "where there is an ongoing consensus among the members of the organization about the purposes of their interaction" (p. 9).

"Does the organization behave? Can 'it' desire?" are questions put forward by Argyris (1964) in *Integrating the Individual and the Organization*. These questions are used as a prelude to his discussion of organizational goals. In Argyris's opinion, organizations have goals. However, these goals are not formulated by any mandator or dominating group of stakeholders, but constitute reactions to several complex processes. "When we say that 'it' is doing something or other we are summarizing a complex state of affairs within the organism in question. In psychology we learn that when we say 'he is perceiving' or 'he is learning to read,' we are summarizing an extremely complex set of interrelated activities not as yet fully understood. The same is true for the group and the organization" (Argyris, 1964, p. 155). The organization is characterized by three forms of activity: (1) achieving objectives, (2) maintaining the internal system, and (3) adapting to the external environment (Argyris, 1964, p.120). According to Argyris, these "core activities" may be found in all organizations.

How does Argyris (1964) characterize the process of goal achievement? Goal-setting activities "are part of the problem-solving process." Again, what is this? Problem solution exists to "help the organization overcome the forces toward organizational ineffectiveness" (p. 145). What is a *problem*? A *problem* may be defined as an external or internal stimulus "that creates a chain reaction of complex events inside the system and upsets the existing steady state of the system" (Argyris, 1964, p. 137).

Goals and goal setting are directly linked to organizational problem solving, a process that is activated as a result of disturbances that affect the system from the inside or from the outside. The implications of Argyris's discussion are the same as those of Katz and Kahn's (1966): *Goals* are treated as a dependent variable, an effect of "complex processes within the system," and thereby, cannot be conceived of as either the starting point for, or cause of, organizational action.

Simon (1947/1957) presents a comparatively goal-directed variant of modern organizational systems theory. For example, he emphasizes that "most organizations are oriented around some goal or objective which provides the purpose toward which the organization's decisions and activities are directed" (p. 112). However, at the same time, he views the organization as a "natural system." In his conception of organizational goals, he approaches the notion that the organizational goal structure is a complex expression of the multitude of goals that are presented by the various participants. At a certain point, this goal structure emerges as a compromise between the interest of the different "potential participants." The organizational goal makes up a kind of least common denominator around which the different groups of participants can be joined. If the organizational goal is not acceptable to a certain individual group, that group will end its cooperation with the organization (Simon, 1947/1957, p. 115).

7

The Rationalistic Perspective: Problems and Shortcomings

Introduction

As the spokesmen of the systems perspective often argue, there are more essential aspects to an organization than its goal-achieving activities. For example, Argyris (1964) stresses that besides goal achievement, the organization has to fulfill certain requirements of integration (preservation has of the inner system) and adaptation (adjustment to the environment). In regard to both of these points, one may argue that the rationalistic perspective is insufficient. It calls attention to questions concerning the suitability and success of the organization as an instrument for its mandator. If one regards the organization as a means for carrying out work this viewpoint is of central importance. However, it is clear that this far from exhausts the problems relevant to organizational life. In this chapter I shall try to cover some of the limitations of the rationalistic perspective. The discussion will contain comments on (1) the limits of implementing the means-end scheme that are derived from the outer conditions for organizational activity, (2) the difference between this type of rationality limitation and those limitations that have been discussed by Simon (1947/1957), (3) some viewpoints concerning an analysis of the informal system carried out by the human relations school, and finally, (4) certain problems relating to the application of the means-ends scheme.

The Limits of Rationality

External Forces

Organizational analysis of the rationalistic type takes its point of departure from the notion that the organization is a product of the plans of an acting subject. The emphasis on goal factors (transformed into recommendations for action through the means-ends scheme) is at one and the same time the strength and weakness of rationalistic theory. The strength lies in its continuous insistence that organizations be regarded as the instruments for implementation of certain objectives. That is, rationalistic theory emphasizes the notion that some actor, here generally labeled the mandator, has a particular interest in the organization's work, and that this actor accordingly can be expected to maintain in different ways his or her superiority over the organization.

The weaknesses in rationalistic theory stem from its inattentiveness to factors that may limit the space for rational choice and planning. It is impossible to conceive of an organization completely without rationalistic components. At the same time, however, it is necessary to realize that rational action is limited by certain frame factors or conditions delimit the space within which action may take place, and which provide the material and economic base for action.

Organizational theory can be subjectivistic only within the field indicated by these factors. How large this field is in reality is a question of much debate and is subject to many arguments of a more or less materialistic-deterministic kind. Sunesson (1974, p. 71) strongly stresses his objections to "all forms of organization-theoretical voluntarism and idealism" and carries his criticism so far that one gets the impression that organizational action is determined almost completely by material factors and/or relations to the state. Berntson (1974), who also argues from an historical-materialistic point of departure, is considerably less categorical when he says that "the action motives of actors, their subjective orientation, plays a definite role" within the framework of "external objective conditions" (p. 35). In general, I agree with Berntson.

Three important classes of conditions limiting subjective rationality are (1) economic, (2) technological, and (3) political frame factors. Economic factors have to do with the availability of land, capital, and labor to the organization; technological factors derive from the development of the productive forces, i.e., the efficiency of machines, means of communication, etc., which are necessary for the daily tasks of the organization; political factors concern the organization's relationship with, and dependence on, the state and other dominating power groups (a dependency that is often codified in laws and statutes; see Chapter 1, "On Rules and Relations"). At the same time that one stresses the importance of incorporating rationalistic assumptions into general organization theory, one has to emphasize the necessity for explicitly taking into account those limitations that stem from the aforementioned frame factors and that circumscribe the goal rationality of actors.

The three classes of conditions that I have mentioned are largely reflected in the organizational structure of society. The economic forces are matched in different organizations for material production: organizations that in a historical perspective increasingly represent capital concentration and the division of labor, from craftsmen to giant corporations.

The development of the forces of productivity toward greater efficiency and technical complexity in the work process gives rise to different categories of technical and administrative specialists such as civil and military engineers, groups of people who have mastered, and been given the opportunity to put to use, the increasing amount of knowledge of the natural sciences in, for example, mechanical engineering, thermodynamics, electromagnetism, optics, chemistry, bacteriology, and biology. In the 1800s, science became more and more professionalized, and the division into basic research and applied research became established. To safeguard their interests—which may be done by making efforts to gain control of the recruitment of new people to the profession and by developing an esprit de corps and ethical rules for the professional group—the experts formed their professional organizations. Clergy, lawyers and physicians, the three classic professions in preindustrial society, had achieved a high degree of professional unity at an early stage. Advances in the natural sciences paved the way for more and more professional associations. Carr-Saunders (1966) gives the following examples from Britain in the 1800s (the year in which the organization was founded is in parentheses).

The Institution of Civil Engineers (1818)
The Royal Institute of British Architects (1834)
The Pharmaceutical Society (1841)
The Royal College of Veterinary Surgeons (1844)
The Institution of Mechanical Engineers (1847).

Society also became more administratively complex: Basic education, for example, rapidly became more widespread and a need for bookkeeping and accounting arose in industry and commerce. In 1870, British teachers formed the National Union of Teachers, and the National Union of Chartered Accountants was formed in 1880 (Carr-Saunders, 1966, p. 3). Thus technical and administrative trends were reflected in the formation of professional associations.

There was also a growing trend toward professionalization in the field of human technology (for example, in medical care and psychiatric care) and in the field of job motivation (for example, industrial psychology and human relations). The conflicts created in society—among other things through the rapid growth of industrial production in combination with an unequal distribution of the results of production, through government administration and taxation interventions and through the conflict of interests between capital owners and people without possessions and between city dwellers and the rural population—are expressed in the formation of political associations. The processes of national unification, the emergence of centralized government power, the concentration of industry, urbanization, and improved communications paved the way for greater collective consciousness in the various social strata: a consciousness that large groups shared common life conditions and that poor working conditions, economic exploitation, and a lack of power were not limited to one's own family or the local community. Demands for general political enfranchisement began to be made of the established social classes, which, in their turn, joined forces even more closely. These processes of struggle, organization, and counterorganization came to be expressed in, among other ways, the formation of political parties and voting associations, which were founded and supported by the working class, the farming community, the progressive bourgeoisie, industrialists, and capitalists.

Economic, technical, and political changes in society are mirrored by the emergence of different types of organization. The organizations are instruments for different mandators with definite interests in bringing about certain changes in society (or that society remains unchanged). Put another way: economic, technical, and political changes lead to changes in society's mandator population, i.e., in the initiators and backers of organizations.

Limits of Human Rationality

A quite different type of rationalistic limitation is emphasized by Simon. In contrast to those frameworks of rational action that are sketched out by Marxist theory (based on assumptions about society), Simon (1947/1957) stresses those limits for complete rationality that are inherent in the *individual*. When Simon talks about the "limits of rationality," he does not primarily refer to factors that limit the freedom of action for the *organization* but for the organization *member.* (The term *member* is Simon's. On the problems of applying it in organizational theory; see Chapter 8, "Who is a 'Member'?").

The knowledge that the individual possesses or is able to acquire is by necessity always fragmentary. It is against this background that the organization becomes important: "One function that organization performs is to place the organization members in a psychological environment that will adapt their decisions to the organization objectives, and will provide them with the information needed to make decisions correctly" (Simon, 1947/1957, p. 79).

Left to themselves, humans are weak and incapable of reaching "correct" decisions, says Simon. Individuals need the support of the organization, which carries out distribution of tasks, decides on how tasks are to be carried out, transmits decisions through its ranks "by establishing systems of authority and influence," and educates and indoctrinates "its members." Through these processes, the organization "injects into the very nervous system of the organization members the criteria of decision that the organization wishes to employ" (Simon, 1947/1957, p. 103). These citations illustrate that the foundation of Simon's perspective on humans is *irrationalism,* rather than rationalism. The organization is perceived of as a means not primarily for overcoming material and structural obstacles to action, but for counteracting tendencies inherent in the individual organizational member that undermine his or her possibilities of reaching "correct" decisions. (A development of this train of thought, with what are at times breathtaking conclusions, is presented by Brunsson, 1985, in *The Irrational Organization*).

Conceptions of Humanity: On "Praxis"

McClosky (1958) has pointed out the links between the irrational concept of individuals and conservative thinking. According to him, the conservative thinking emphasizes the unpredictability of human action and its tendencies to anarchy. A conservative person is apt to stress the need for strengthening social institutions, law, and order. "Order, authority, and community are the primary defense against the impulse of violence and anarchy" (McClosky, 1958). Simon's (1947/1957) idea of the limitations of rational behavior inherent in the individual offers an excellent motive for defending the role of authority within organizations. If the individual cannot be expected to reach completely rational decisions, he or she is supplied with the means for this by the organization. The latter is expected to be more rational than the individual organizational member. According to Simon (1947/1957), the behavior pattern of the subordinate is governed by the decision criterion to "follow that behavior alternative which is selected for me by the superior" (p. 126).

It may be interesting to contrast the perspective of humanity as exhibited by Simon with conceptions represented by humanistic Marxism. According to the latter, the subject is treated as an "active, creative, consciously acting individual" (Israel, 1972, p. 44). The individual is seen as possessing an active, expansive mind. Practical activity, *praxis,* is an important condition for achieving and expanding his or her knowledge (cf., Israel, 1971, p. 84ff.).

The rationalistic undertone in Marxism is also well illustrated by the following well-known quotation from *Capital:*

> A spider conducts operations which resemble those of the weaver, and a bee would put many a human architect to shame by the construction of the honeycomb cells. But what distinguishes the worst architect from the best of the bees is that the architect builds the cell in his mind before he constructs it in wax. At the end of every labour process, a result emerges which had already been conceived by the worker at the beginning, hence already existed ideally. (Marx, 1976, p. 284)

In sum, one may argue that Marxism's concept of humanity and the rationalistic approach to organizations are quite compatible if one explicitly takes into consideration those material conditions that delimit and circumscribe the individual's actions (cf. Sjoberg & Nett, 1968, pp. 62-63). The process model developed in Chapter 9 combines elements of rationalistic theory with assumptions concerning the material limits to rationality.

The Informal System

An obvious and justified point of critique against rationalistic theory is its inattention to most informal group formations that emerge within organizations. That is groups which arise outside the blueprint drawn up by the organizational mandator are not adequately discussed within rationalistic theory. Proponents of scientific management ideas concentrate their observations on the formal organization, and attempt to make it as perfect as possible. The correct distribution of work and central coordination were to Taylor (1969) the keys to good organization and high productivity. If the workers made agreements among themselves with the purpose of reducing work pace, this was a disturbance in the smoothness of production that Taylor simply could not accept. "It should be plain to all men . . . that this deliberate loafing is almost criminal," he growls (p. 96).

The first important break with the scientific management ideology and its emphasis on the formal principles of job distribution came with Roethlisberger and Dickson's (1947) Western Electric studies. Because of their research contributions, organizations increasingly came to be described as social systems in which the informal relations of the employees—their feelings, their values, their early history, and their relations to groups outside of the organization (e.g., their families)—became important analytical components. "There is something more to the social organization than what has been formally recognized," wrote Roethlisberger and Dickson (1947). "The blueprint plans of the company show the functional relations between working units, but they do not express the distinctions of social distance, movement, or equilibrium previously described." And: "Man is not merely—in fact is very seldom—motivated by factors pertaining strictly to facts or logic" (pp. 54-55). One conclusion that has been drawn from this study, which has stimulated further research, is that informal organization, if correctly used, can be employed to support the goals of the enterprise. Conversely, if employees have goals of their own that are contradictory to those of the enterprise, coordination and communication are obstructed (Roethlisberger & Dickson, 1947, p. 57).

Since the publication of *Management and the Worker* (Roethlisberger & Dickson, 1947), a vast number of analyses have focused on the human relations aspect of organizations. It is not an overstatement to say that the human relations tradition has dominated, for example, Swedish sociological research on enterprises and organizations during the 1940s and 1950s (see, e.g., Boalt, 1954; Boalt & Westerlund, 1953; Dahlström, 1956; Lundquist, 1957; Segerstedt & Lundquist, 1952).

The human relations approach has primarily been used for the research analysis of the lower levels of the enterprise. Roethlisberger and Dickson (1947) distinguish between, on the one hand, the logic of cost and efficiency, which is said to characterize the enterprise leadership, and, on the other, the logic of sentiment that governs the employees. As Gouldner (1959) stresses, the goal-oriented strivings of the employees tend to be seen as not rational in themselves, but "as a façade for their own underlying non-rational needs" (p. 407). Like Simon's approach, the analysis of Roethlisberger and Dickson emphasizes that employees within an organization should be treated primarily as nonrational actors.

The Application of Means-Ends Analysis: Some Problems

The practical employment of a means-ends analysis is complicated by several factors. A short recapitulation will make this clear. (1) The means-ends method is based on the supposition that it is possible to construct a coherent means-ends hierarchy in which supergoals and subgoals are logically connected with each other. In actual practice, these demands are seldom completely fulfilled. (2) On all goal levels, implementation requires that the goals be so well specified that they can be transformed into programs for action (i.e., operationalized) without too much difficulty. This puts high demands on the persons responsible for planning, and failures in this respect can lead to discontent and criticism from those who are to carry out the program. (3) Finally, there is considerable risk that *efficiency* will be too narrowly defined with the result that short-sighted productivity goals are emphasized at the cost of more wide-ranging objectives. I shall comment on some of the problems connected with these three points in the rest of this chapter.

"Organizations Do Not Reach Their Goals"

It is almost trivial to point out that decision making in real situations often looks quite different from what is designed in rationalistic blueprint. Simon's (1947/1957) observations concerning the difficulty of achieving a complete overview of the goals and action alternatives can hardly be questioned. Individuals satisfy instead of optimize. That is, they choose between available acceptable alternatives rather than look for what is best by absolute standards.

When Etzioni (1964, pp. 16-17) maintains that organizations rarely reach their goals, he seems to take his point of departure from an optimalization model. It is true that organizations often do not reach their ultimate goals, but this does not mean that the organization does not approach these goals. To take just one example, the Swedish trade union movement in its program of 1886 defined its goals as "protecting the workers against the repression and despotism of employers, and step by step to guarantee all members of society complete human and citizen rights" (Gunnarsson, 1965, p. 62). It can be disputed to what extent this goal has been reached. But it can hardly be disputed that the success of the organization, at least partly, can be measured by studying how different subgoals, which are related to the more ultimate ones, have been reached. Many of the necessary steps or subgoals specified by the program have been achieved. For example, the reduction of working hours, general health insurance, old-age pensions, general and equal voting rights, progressive income tax, and general basic education. Although supergoals are often vague, they can still be essential components in the formulation of organizational aspirations.

It can be somewhat pointless to criticize an organization for not achieving its supergoals. Yet it is a reasonable request that lower goal levels can clarify the general purposes and that the lower-level goals are specific enough to allow controls of whether they have been carried out (e.g., the subgoal, "8-hour working day").

Emphasizing the superordinate goals at the expense of an analysis of the way they are expressed as concrete instructions for action may mean that the best (the superordinate goal) becomes the enemy of the good (the concrete action). The total rejection of the concept of goals as a basis for organization studies—which has on occasion been suggested—is to needlessly forego a good aid. The goals of organizations are not always uniform—but they may be a good point of departure from which to ask oneself why they are not.

Objectives may be vague or contradictory if they are the product of contradictions between different rationalities. Unlike the efforts of the human relation school to define different rationalities at different levels in the company—where the use of concepts like *the logic of feeling* is a tacit affirmation of the incapacity of the employees—the distinction between rationalities based on different interests may be important here. A negotiation situation arises when, for example, company management interests (expressed in goals such as increased profits) are set against employees' interests (expressed in goals such as higher pay or better working conditions).

To summarize: Criticism of the rationalistic model is justified if the model is perceived as a direct straight-line relationship between goals and means. Reality is seldom as simple as that. This is, however, not sufficient reason to reject research on the goals of organizations. Goals act as symbols and driving forces for organized work, and even if they are not achieved in full, they are an expression of the mandate under which the executive and employees work. This mandate is, in turn, an important point of departure for research into the micropolitics of the organization. Furthermore, the analysis of conflicts in the organization often benefits from being carried on in terms of existing goals inasmuch as the internal opposition often expresses its demands by promoting alternatives to established goals. *Goals* thus become a portal to research and the legitimation of the power structure and challenges to it, and to research into the history of the organization. It is not the static but the mutable aspects of the goals that are the most interesting from the organization theoretical viewpoint (cf. Clegg & Dunkerley, 1980, p. 333).

Problems of Method

Concretization of Goals. One of the basic problems of the rationalistic model is its inability to formulate goals that are specific enough to allow the researcher to determine whether they have been reached or not. As I argued earlier, the existence of diffuse supergoals is not a sufficient reason for rejecting the means-ends analysis.

The loose connection between supergoals and lower-level goals shows, however, that insufficient goal specification can have direct effects on values. There are no established neutral methods to logically deduce specific subgoals from ultimate goals. Thus the application of means-ends analysis will always have consequences of an evaluative nature, even at lower levels in an organization. For example, it is naive to believe that politically elected representatives make choices concerning goals, whereas the tasks of administrators in an organization (e.g., the state apparatus) are only to implement these goals. As Dahlström (1971, pp. 66ff.), among others, has pointed out, the choice of means (subgoals) can never be conceived of as a completely neutral process.

Measurability, Effectiveness, and Efficiency. The discussion above directs our attention to another problem: that those who are entrusted with the implementation of a program may find the general goals so diffuse that they concentrate their work on activities that have easily and directly measurable results. There is a considerable risk that organizational activities will concentrate only on goals that are concrete and possible to operationalize, at the cost of goals that are more abstract and for which success criteria are less clear (cf., Etzioni, 1964, p. 9).

The problem may be expressed in terms of *effectiveness* and *efficiency,* two terms that are conceptually separate. As Etzioni (1964, p. 8) points out, *effectiveness* concerns the goal achievement of the organization, whereas *efficiency* represents the relation between a certain activity and the costs of its execution. Measurements of efficiency concern the costs of carrying out a specific task. Such productivity measurements can be implemented quite independent of any evaluation of the implementation of supergoals. That is, an organization may fulfill criteria of efficiency without being effective in goal-achievement terms. It is not, however, possible to conceive of an organization that fulfills criteria of effectiveness while at the same time being 100% inefficient. A certain degree of efficiency is a necessary but not sufficient condition for effectiveness.

For purposes of illustration, let us look at the following example. The effectiveness of the Swedish State Bacteriological Laboratory (SBL) concerns SBL's contributions to the improvement of public health. Among its responsibilities is the production of vaccines to prevent the dissemination of contagious diseases. One measure of SBL's efficiency is provided by the volume of vaccine that SBL is producing and the costs of these operations (RRV, 1971, p. 73). It is obvious that there is not a perfect fit between this one productivity measure and the demands of effectiveness put to the SBL and those that are formulated in the statutes of the laboratory. If the SBL were 100% inefficient in its production of vaccines, its more general goal of promoting public health could not be implemented (assuming that vaccines are necessary for the public health programs).

8

The Systems Perspective: Problems and Shortcomings

Introduction

The emphasis that the human relations school placed on the informal system represented a reaction against the practice within the scientific management tradition of concentrating on the formal aspects of work distribution. The systems approach that owed much to the human relations tradition meant a paradigmatic change in organizational sociology. It posed questions that, if answered, required a simultaneous consideration of *both* the informal *and* the formal system of organization. A new set of relevant questions developed: Which are the strategic parts of the system? How are these parts interrelated? By which processes is the adjustment of the various parts to each other achieved? Reciprocal relations, systems balance, and system adjustment were the new key words. One may perhaps argue that organizational theory has acquired its necessary synthesis in this process. Certain elements from the original, strongly "machine-directed" scientific management theory have been preserved. For example, its emphasis on the distribution and coordination of work will in all probability be continuous elements in social science analyses of organizations. The human relations school has so effectively pointed out the need for studying the social organization, informal group formation, communication, and information that its contributions will undoubtedly continue to be important to organizational theory. Finally, general systems theory has indicated the possibility of combining the two approaches in a common perspective, emphasizing the importance of studying the organization as a whole, its functions, balance, integration, and adjustment.[1] Is there, in fact, any reason to demand more? Is there any reason to search for alternatives?

I believe there is. In large measure, the systems perspective has managed to conceal the major point of rationalistic analysis: the thesis that *the organization exists to carry out tasks for the benefit of a mandator.* It has done so under the pretext of presenting a holistic analysis of the organization within the framework of open systems theory. The countercurrent, which has existed at various times, has had few possibilities of being heard over the pressures of these claims and ambitions.[2] Self-criticism among systems theoreticians has not been a particularly striking phenomenon.

In this chapter, I shall present some critical points related to the systems perspective. These criticisms are directed at the conceptual apparatus of systems theory, its views of organizational history, its propositions about dominance relationships in the organization, its basic thesis of inducement-contribution balance, and finally, problems related to its employment of the concept of *member.*

The Conceptual Apparatus

The conceptual apparatus of systems theory is developed for the purpose of creating a general theory of so-called vitalistic systems (i.e., human organisms, groups, organizations, and societies; see Blegen & Nyléhn, 1969, p. 9ff.). (Cf. Buckley, 1967, "The major concern is with models of organization sufficiently general and complex, though built from simple units, to embrace behavior systems of any type—physical, biological, psychological, or socio-cultural," p. 4.) The proponents of the systems perspective claim that it has the ability to interpret and formulate propositions concerning a multitude of different empirical phenomena of an open-systems character in terms of input, output, feedback, equilibrium, relative openness/closedness, environmental requirements, adaptation, energy input, energy transformation, etc.

The general adaptability of the systems approach is probably one of the main explanations of its wide popularity within the social and behavioral sciences. Another probable reason is its suitability for mathematical formalization by the use of differential calculus and set theory (see, e.g., Norrbom, 1971, pp. 7ff.). Acceptance of the systems perspective is partly dependent on one's belief in the practical applicability of its conceptual apparatus. It also partly hinges on one's confidence in the possibilities of creating a general, formalized theory using the aforementioned methods. On this point I wish to stress my own general skepticism. Organizational systems theory has, as yet, produced few, if any, formal mathematical models capable of explaining and predicting organizational behavior.

The generality of the systems concept represents a considerable weakness. In their efforts to develop a general theory, the spokespeople for the systems perspective often extend the meaning of terms so far as to render them vague and impossible to specify in operational terms. Let me exemplify this by reviewing the use of the concept of energy in organizational systems theory. *Energy* in the systems tradition is logically connected with, among other things, the concept of efficiency.

Energy and Efficiency

Systems theory strives to measure the total energy input to an organization. If this cannot be achieved, the concept of efficiency becomes less useful, because efficiency is related to the organization's way of distributing the energy intake. As long as we stick to, for example, mechanical energy, the difficulties are not insurmountable, although still considerable. It is probably possible to construct useful measures of that energy that is generated when humans and machines work on the material that is brought into the organization's production system. Also, other forms of physical energy that the organization employs may be measured, e.g., its import of electric energy.

A substantial problem is, however, that the efficiency of organizations can usually be only partially explained by measurable production factors. There remains a large amount of variation that is related to factors that are private, i.e., inherent in each individual, or that are produced when the individuals in the organization cooperate and interact. Let me illustrate with the following example.

Economists strive to explain the increase of the gross national product (GNP) by, for example, adding up the increments in the amount of productive work accomplished plus the growth of physical capital. The summation of these measurable factors, however, explains only a limited portion of the total increase of the GNP (see, e.g., *SOU,* 1966, pp. 1, 18-19). "Human capital factors," like the increase of knowledge, improved health, human creativity, and efficiency increases due to better organization, have to be included as a part of the unexplained residual (Schulz, 1971). It is possible that a large amount of the variation in productivity between different organizations can be explained in a similar way.

How would a systems theorist measure the energy intake and energy transformation of an organization? Katz and Kahn (1966) explain, after a longer discussion of the problem, that a comprehensive measure does not in fact exist: the measure that may be used in estimating energy factors is primarily their value in money (dollars). And this, they say in a somewhat defeatist manner, "is not necessarily commensurate with energic input and output" (p. 152). I find it easy to agree with them. It should be added that for many organizations that are not occupied with commodity production, the problem of measurement is especially difficult.

In *Integrating the Individual and the Organization,* Argyris (1964) attempts to take into consideration propositions concerning "human capital" and human energy. The organization, he states, exists partially to use the "psychological energy" of the individual, energy that "is hypothesized to increase as the individual's experiences of psychological success increase, and to decrease with psychological failure" (Argyris, 1964, p. 33). The problem of the operationalization of this concept, however, is solved somewhat too simply by Argyris. He frankly states that the existence of the concept of psychological energy "does not depend on its being located in the empirical world (as may be the case for physiological energy)" (p. 22).

> The acceptance of the construct of psychological energy will be a function of its (1) logical validity, which, in turn, is a function of its internal consistency as well as its relevance in a conceptual scheme and, (2) its power to help explain human behavior. (Argyris, 1964, p. 22)

But neither 1 nor 2 is any argument for the empirical usefulness of systems theory and the concept of psychological energy. One may appreciate a theoretical construction for its logical qualities. One may even agree that the concept of psychological energy is a possible partial explanation of the efficiency of organizations. However, as long as it is not possible to determine the kind and amount of this postulated energy (like many other concepts in systems theory), the systems perspective has not proved to be superior to, for example, a rationalistic theory based on goal evaluation.

The Doctrine of Harmony

System-based theories of the enterprise and similarly, system-based theories of work motivation, have been extensively discussed and criticized not only in social science but in political debates as well. The critique has been largely directed against the harmony perspective of the systems approach. For example, Krupp (1961, p. xi) uses the concept *organization theory* (as distinct from *administrative design theory,* i.e., scientific management) to include human relations in industry, small group theory, and especially, the writings of Barnard and Simon.

> Together these points of departure form a logically connected body of theory with a common emphasis founded in the norm of cooperation and harmony.

As a consequence, these theories frame a managerial point of view in the traditions of philosophic conservatism and management engineering. Organization theory forms part of a larger, more general, managerial interpretation of society. (p. xi)

Below, I shall briefly touch on some of the effects of the harmony thesis. My purpose is not primarily to show how conflicts of interest in the organization are concealed, as this follows almost as a matter of definition. It is rather to point out the connection between the frequently loose concepts of systems theory and the manipulative consequences that can follow.

Argyris (1964, pp. 170ff.) argues for the humanization of enterprises through the abolition of authoritarian leadership, the introduction of more liberal principles of enterprise management, increased codetermination, job rotation, etc. For these reasons, he takes a stand against "the pyramidal structure" (i.e., a mechanistic type of organization) and recommends a "healthy organization" (i.e., one with an organic character; Argyris, 1964, p. 133). This type of organization is characterized by, among other things, the absence of labor conflicts (pp. 189-190).

The discontent of workers in enterprises is often channeled via trade unions. The existence of such associations, however, is detrimental to organizational health: "The introduction of trade unions tends to develop stress within an organization at first" (Argyris, 1964, p. 131). But unions are also a mixed blessing in the long run. If one attempts, as Argyris has, to create an organic type of organization, trade unions become an obstacle because of their pyramidal, hierarchic structure. For Argyris (1964), the creation of a trade union is a method of adjustment for workers; however,

the irony of this mode of adaptation is that the union also organizes itself by using the pyramidal structure. Now, the worker may become doubly dependent and subordinate. (p. 61)

The relationship between trade unions and management may be either good or poor. Poor relations are characterized by, among other things, the trade union ignoring the interdependence of relationships in the enterprise, and keeping management in the dark about its strategy (Argyris, 1964, p. 189). Good relations, however, have the property of keeping communication channels open, with both parties working toward constructive solutions. Argyris cites industrial research by Whyte (1956), summarizing Whyte's results by saying: "In terms of our model, we would say that the interdependence of parts by both parties was recognized, influence of the parts on the whole (labor-management system) was significantly increased, as was the time perspective" (Argyris, 1964, p. 190). The equilibrium of the system can thus be disturbed, first, by the employees' establishing an organization of their own, and second, by the use of traditional trade union means of influence.

It would be pointless to deny the main thesis that the equilibrium of the system is disturbed as a result of such processes. If one confines oneself to the view that the mutual interdependence of parts requires the absence of interest organizations, and that trade unions tend to be associated with conflicts ("a worker possessing favorable attitudes toward the union tended to have unfavorable attitudes toward work" according to one survey cited by Argyris, 1964, p. 63), the conclusion follows almost automatically: The balance is necessarily disturbed and the organization's health is threatened.

Finally, in this section a note is required on Argyris's view of the positive results that can be achieved through job enlargement, codetermination, and increase in the worker's responsibility for his job. Argyris quotes a study by Melman, showing positive results from the introduction of self-managing work groups. One of the advantages, according to Argyris (1964), was that "under conditions of increased work responsibility, management was freed to focus more on marketing problems (and other problems with the environment). Also the need for foremen was greatly reduced and their work responsibilities become radically changed" (p. 237).

Thus reductions in detailed control mean better resource management. Argyris expresses this as a gain in the effectiveness of the system as a whole. This view can be accepted as long as one avoids the question of what the mandator of the organization expects from the "system," and as long as the organization is not analyzed in terms of interests (or rationality/counterrationality). If one takes the latter approach, the question arises as to who benefits the most from increases in productivity.

I am not arguing that changes in the work organization toward greater autonomy for the worker, less supervision, job rotation, etc. are meaningless reforms. The humanization of work environment may be justified even if it does not involve any great step toward increased influence for the employees over the organization's management. It is important, however, that one does not confuse *quantitative* changes, which increase work control, with reforms that lead to a *qualitative* change in the basic power relations in the enterprise., i.e., a change of mandator.

Walter Buckley: Microtheory, Morphogenesis, and the System as Actor

The perhaps most influential contribution to systems thinking in the social sciences during the last decade is Buckley's (1967) *Sociology and Modern Systems Theory*. Buckley attacks equilibrium and homeostatic-organismic models, such as the "social physics" of the 18th and early 19th centuries and functionalist theory. He seeks to replace them with a model emphasizing dynamic processes of organization. He develops a theory that includes considerations of conflict, tension, and system-environmental interplay: the *process,* or *complex adaptive system model.*

> [This model] applies to systems characterized by the elaboration or evolution of organization; as we shall see, they thrive on, in fact depend on, "disturbances" and "variety" in the environment. (Buckley, 1967, p. 40)

Buckley (1967) develops his theory by proceeding gradually from small, relatively uncomplicated elements to more complex and elaborated phenomena:

> This development proceeds from the micro-level of the act and the basic symbolic interaction process . . . to the more or less stabilized interaction matrix referred to the *role* and role dynamics, to the complex of roles contributing to the makeup of *organizations* and *institutions.* (p. 82)

Elements are related to each other by means of *information.* Information is important, because it is the carrier of *meaning.* Society, according to Buckley (1967), may be described as "an organization of meanings" (p. 92).

> In general, we find that meanings are generated in a process of social interaction of a number of individuals dealing with a more or less common environment. Once generated, they act in the capacity of selective functions underlying the decision-making processes that make possible (but do not guarantee) organized social behavior. (Buckley, 1967, p. 94)

In Buckley's model, the concept of morphogenesis is strategic. *Morphogenesis* refers to processes that tend to elaborate or change a system's form, structure, or state; i.e., biological evolution, learning, and societal development. This is in contrast to pattern-preservation or *morphostasis,* exemplified by Buckley (1967) as "homeostatic processes in organisms, and ritual in socio-cultural systems" (pp. 58-59). Strain and tension are natural, in fact essential, elements in morphogenesis: "We must view *tension* as a normal, ever-present dynamic agent which . . . must . . . be kept at an optimal level if the system is to remain viable" (Buckley, 1967, p. 160). Thus the main assumptions of consensus theory are questioned by Buckley.

Buckley has presented a critique of traditional, equilibrium-functionalist thinking and an alternative model for the social sciences, which beyond any doubt will rank among the classical contributions. But, although critical of harmony and equilibrium assumptions, his model has certain problematic traits that limit its usefulness for the study of organization processes.

First, the basis of Buckley's model is behavioral *microtheory,* i.e., psychology and social psychology. Buckley (1967) commends, e.g., the exchange theories of Homans and Blau for the reason that they avoid "structural terminology and static categorization." Instead, "they have gone back to basics, starting from scratch with the basic interaction process" and ideas such as "Bentham's 'felicific calculus' " and "Adam Smith's laws of private profit and loss" (p. 127). What Bentham and Smith did, among other things, was to revitalize the classical hedonistic notions of pain and pleasure. These concepts are paralleled in current stimulus-response (S-R) theory by the concepts of *reward* and *cost.* (One may question whether Buckley's, 1967, model really represents a critical alternative to S-R theory, as he implies, p. 95, or whether his theory is only a slight modification of it.) These concepts also constitute the basic building blocks in the Barnard-Simon-March theory of organization, i.e., the *inducement-contribution balance.*

The problems connected with hedonistic, profit maximization assumptions—especially concerning their empirical testability—apply also to Buckley's model. Although starting from scratch is a quite common procedure in current organization theory, it is not necessarily a recommendable procedure. Whereas Buckley (1967, pp. 105-113) approves of Homans's theory because of its basis in psychological propositions, I believe that these very propositions represent fundamental obstacles to developing the theory into a logically strict and empirically fruitful scheme. (More about this will follow in "The Inducement-Contribution Balance," below; see also the discussion on microrationality in Abrahamsson, 1993, chap. 10).

Second, one may ask whether the emphasis on small-group processes does not, in fact, slant the theory toward *centripetal,* equilibrium-sustaining assumptions and toward an emphasis on stability and harmony in spite of Buckley's attempts to represent both centripetal and centrifugal tendencies in his theory.

The small group has provided an atomic unit for social science; and social psychology has aspired to become a science of precise measurement, cleared of normative constraints, proper in its use of rigorous methods (and it is hence attractive to system-theory builders, who often have logical-positivist, unity-of-science ambitions; cf. Krupp, 1961, p. 123). Buckley's theory is biased toward overstating the role of the social atom and, in doing this, tends to overlook some of the very organizational conflict phenomena it attempts to model. To use Krupp's (1961) formulation:

> Small group theory and a psychological orientation may seriously understate the actual interdependence between members at any given organization level

(plant slow-down), significant discontinuities (wildcat strikes), and codification (unions). Euclidean geometry is being used, perhaps, in a non-Euclidean world. Tying a theory of organization behavior to theories of individual motion and decision (or to small group behavior) severely limits its predictive and explanatory capabilities. (p. 166)

What Krupp stresses is the danger of losing sight of *collective organization* based on *common interests* among particular groups of actors *confronting* each other rather than cooperating, or, in other words, tendencies that are not only centrifugal but perhaps so centrifugal as to render the notion of a system fruitless.

It is easy to find formulations by Buckley which may cause the reader to question the "conflict sensitivity" of his theory. For example, he states:

Modern systems analysis suggests that a sociocultural system with high adaptive potential, or integration as we might call it, requires some optimum level of both stability and flexibility: a relative stability of the social-psychological foundations of interpersonal relations and of the cultural meanings and value-hierarchies that hold group members together in the same universe of discourse and, at the same time, a flexibility of structural relations characterized by the lack of strong barriers to change, along with a certain propensity for reorganizing the current institutional structure should environmental challenges or emerging internal conditions suggest the need. (Buckley, 1967, p. 206)

One may ask: Who sets the criteria for the "optimum level of stability?" According to whom do the "sociopsychological foundations of interpersonal relations" fulfill requirements of "relative stability?" According to what standards is there "sameness" in the universe of discourse? And how do we recognize the "suggestions" for reorganization by "environmental challenges or emerging internal conditions?"

Systems theory, however critical of earlier approaches it aspires to be, cannot escape from the fundamental idea of the system as actor and, thereby, from the implication that individuals or groups of actors in the system are subordinated to forces essentially beyond their control. Systems theory is biased toward underrepresenting human rationality; it tends to attribute "human" characteristics to the system as a whole, i.e., it has an anthropomorphic, or animistic, bias. Of course, independent action by subunits is assumed away already at the stage of defining the system as an *interrelation* of parts. Thus the system is seen as the acting subject, adapting itself to internal and external requirements and setting its own criteria for stability, flexibility, "optimum level of tension," etc.

This bias of anthropomorphism is reflected, for example, in the very title of Katz and Kahn's (1966) book *The Social Psychology of Organizations,* in the vast literature on "organizational psychology" and "organizational development" (see, e.g., Back, 1972), and is a prominent feature in the writings of Argyris (e.g., 1964).

How justified is the assumption of the system as actor when we deal with, e.g., the industrial enterprise? Are not the interests and resources vested in different groups in the organization and the perhaps conflicting goals sought by them as actors, more fruitful starting points for organizational research? Does not the notion of the system as actor necessarily lead us to investigations concerning the conditions for the system's maintenance, thereby directing our attention away from the life-conditions of the people within it?

Although Buckley certainly has the ambition to present a systems theory that includes aspects of power, conflict, and tension, this ambition leaves meager results in regard to the reasons for and actual functioning of conflicts. Abstract, formal, and technological aspects of the system are stressed at the expense of the concrete problems that groups and individuals meet and at the expense of the reasons for organization that actors within the system may have, and the types of constraints that may limit attempts to organization. Buckley's theory is almost completely devoid of subject content; it is, to quote Krupp (1961), very much a kind of "Euclidian geometry" in a "non-Euclidian world."

Reification

When systems theory draws a parallel between humans and materials (the concept of energy does not distinguish between these two kinds of production factors), it leads to consequences that are directly opposed to the liberal views of the human relations school, consequences that may involve a dehumanized view of man. Somewhat strangely, this appears very clearly in two books that deal with organization in which the humanitarian aspects would seem to be among the most important, i.e., hospitals. Let me exemplify with Rhenman's (1969) *The Central Hospital (Centrallasarettet)*, and Asplund's (1973) *Health Care Administration (Sjukvårdsadministration)*, which is a further development of Rhenman's theory.

Rhenman sees the hospital as a system of *components*. The components are, for example, the different hospital departments, their wards and the service organs connected to them, and the various positions within these units (doctor, psychologist, almoner, work therapist, physiotherapist, etc.). Among other things, the behavior of the components is influenced by information. Bits of information that affect behavior are called *controlling impulses* (Rhenman, 1969, p. 25; 1967, p. 6). The hospital may be described as a *controlled production system,* containing *administrative* and *productive units.* The administrative components have as their "sole task to . . . transform and transport information and thereby govern the flow of resources into and out of the hospital and the production within the hospital" (Rhenman, 1969, pp. 24-25). The hospital has two main products, outpatient and inpatient care (p. 196). It offers a product assortment consisting of the different types of treatment and care (p. 118). What is called production planning in industry is represented in the hospital by "intake planning and actual intake." Similarly, "production preparation" has a parallel in the hospital's decisions on treatment (pp. 198-199).

Rhenman (1969) recommends and employs himself "an industrial conceptual apparatus" (p. 196) for the analysis of public organizations in general and, in particular, the hospital. This apparatus reaches its technological peak in Asplund's (1973) book on health care administration. As early as a heading in the introductory chapter, the points of association with Rhenman are clearly seen: "The Hospital—An Enterprise." Later on, Asplund (1973) presents a definition of his own of the systems concept of component. According to him, a *component* may be "a group of individuals, a single individual, a group of machines, a single machine, or a combination of individuals and machines" (Asplund, 1973, p. 118). The most interesting components "are quite naturally those . . . which consist of individuals" (p. 120). What properties do they have?

> A component possesses, besides an inner driving force and an ability to receive impulses from the outside, a certain capability to perform, a capability which often is measurable. A component has the ability to carry out, e.g., certain arithmetical operations, to control in an acceptable way certain instruments during a certain time period, to carry out certain manual operations within a given time period, etc. (p. 122)

Different types of individuals/components require different types of guidance and control. This is especially true of the components "problem solvers" and "program executors." The former have "an ability to solve certain problems on the basis of a limited access to information" and, therefore, can be left on their own to some degree. The latter, however, have "an ability to act only on the basis of a very specific order" (Asplund, 1973, p. 122).

Thus the control of a hospital attendant or a patient (for all, according to the theory, are components) is roughly comparable with the control of a somewhat complicated robot. A failure of control depends on faulty information exchange, a lack of ability of the component (cf. Simon's thesis of limited rationality), or in Rhenman's (1967) formulation, "a lack of authority of the sender" (p. 14). March and Simon (1958, p. 54) use the term *machine model* to describe scientific management's view of organizations. In the same way, the picture that emerges from the pages of Rhenman's and Asplund's books is also the picture of a machine. The hospital is described in terms of an industrialized and computerized production system, lacking in almost all forms of *human* relations. It is a system in which the main problems are to get the patients ready for treatment (prepare them for production), treat them (i.e., produce medical care), and put them on the transport line for completed products. Both books were written to be textbooks for the education of health care personnel and for politicians and administrators on local and regional levels. Hence, this narrow, productivity-inspired concept of efficiency may be expected to influence day-to-day medical care situations.

The Stakeholder Model and the Organization's History

The perception of the organization as a system, responsive to stakeholders' needs and striving toward equilibrium and adjustment to its environment, leads to a marked lack of interest in the history of the organization. Questions dealing with, for example, the emergence of the organization, its original initiators, the purposes for which the organization was once created—all of which may be essential for the understanding of the organization's present role and activity—are not considered to be strategic in a systems analysis. The function of the organization *in the presently existing total system* is emphasized at the cost of attempts to explain its present role partly against the background of its formation and development.

Of course, the lack of attention to these factors may be explained by the fact that the various authors do not judge the history of organizations as being particularly interesting for the problems they have chosen to concentrate on. However, when one realizes that a major portion of systems authors avoid this question,[3] one begins to look for other possible reasons. I believe the explanation is that the systems perspective simply functions as an obstacle against an analysis in historical terms.

March and Simon's (1958) theory, based as it is on assumptions about individual motivation, emphasizes the here-and-now factors relevant to organizational equilibrium. If we were to leave this psychological, decision-making, problem-solving framework, we would enter quite another arena, i.e., "the world of strategic factors associated with combat in many fields of battle." But "the March and Simon analysis offers us few tools for this research and no hope of achieving this type of knowledge, particularly since their attempts to measure are restricted to carefully conditioned laboratory experimentation. They have ignored centuries of highly documented instances of economic, social, and political conditions for conflict taken from the concrete records of government and industry. If their analysis is correct there would never be a union" (Krupp, 1961, p. 164).

If one raises the question of the emergence and development of an organization, the systems perspective is prone to give a vague answer that points to these factors as being dependent on the needs of the larger surrounding system. If one sees historical analysis as essential for the study of organizations, these shortcomings of the systems perspective are too pronounced to ignore. The systems-stakeholder theory does not explain how stakeholders have come to be tied to the organization.

Authority Instead of Power

The general importance attached to balance and equilibrium criteria by the systems perspective results in rather diminished attention being directed to the differences in power between various groups and strata in the organization. In fact, the writers in the tradition very often avoid the concept of power altogether, preferring the term *authority* when they discuss relations between superordinates and subordinates in the organization. Briefly, the differences between power and authority are the following: In general, power has to do with the overcoming of resistance within social science literature, there are many variations on this definition. Some authors determine power as the *actual* overcoming of resistance, whereas others define the concept as the capacity to do so. A much-quoted definition is Blalock's (1967), which treats power as a multiplicative function of resources and mobilization. In order for power to exist, a certain degree of both these elements is required. For example, the strike weapon alone does not create a strike. It has to be mobilized, i.e., utilized by some actor who is motivated to use it, who expects that he or she will have at least some success, and who has some concrete objective to achieve through his actions. Mobilization is motivated behavior (see also Abrahamsson, 1972, chap. 12).

Blalock's definition stimulates questions of the following types. Who attempts to overcome whose resistance? Which resources for the overcoming of resistance do the parties in the conflict situation have? In which ways, and on what grounds, do the parties attempt to use (i.e., mobilize) their power resources?

The key concept of systems theory as it describes dominance relationships in an organization is *authority.* A detailed discussion of this concept may be found in Simon's (1947/1957) *Administrative Behavior.* His definition in turn, is based on Barnard's (1968, pp. 163ff.) *The Functions of the Executive* (cf. also, March & Simon, 1958, pp. 99, 161, 167; Ramström, 1964, pp. 35ff.; Rhenman, 1967, p. 16). Simon (1947/1957) defines authority in the following way:

> A subordinate is said to accept authority whenever he permits his behavior to be guided by the decision of a superior, without independently examining the merits of that decision. (pp. 11-12)

Taken literally, this definition may seem almost identical to the concept of power. It obviously concerns a relationship in which the overcoming of resistance may become important, i.e., to get someone to accept authority. Note, however, that the criterion is *consent*. A subordinate "permits" his behavior to be "guided." Simon (1947/1957) is eager to emphasize that the exertion of authority "is usually liberally admixed with suggestion and persuasion" (pp. 11-12). And: "Although it is an important function of authority to permit a decision to be made and carried out even when agreement cannot be reached, perhaps this arbitrary aspect of authority has been overemphasized" (p. 12).

If the superordinate tries to force authority over a certain limit, i.e., the subordinate's *zone of acceptance,* the consequence may be insubordination. What, then, is the zone of acceptance? It is that zone "within which the subordinate is willing to accept the decisions made for him by his superior" (Simon, 1947/1957, p. 133).

Which factors determine the scope of the zone of acceptance? Simon (1947/1957) makes a new attempt at a definition based on the properties of different organizations. "A voluntary organization with poorly defined objectives has perhaps the narrowest range of acceptance. An army, where the sanctions as well as the customs are of extreme severity, has the broadest area of acceptance" (pp. 102-103). Note the subtle vocabulary. A "broad area of acceptance" represents a great *willingness* of the single individual to accept a decision. Thus it does not primarily concern the use of *force* on the part of the organization, and "the sanctions as well as the customs" become means to extend the zone of acceptance of the single person, not primarily means for the organization to exert power.

The role of authority in organizations is to provide a basis for individual decisions, to give premises for the various actions and opinions of individuals (Simon, 1947/1957, pp. 123ff.). In contrast to power, the concept of authority implies that the individual actually is able to make a choice, i.e., between to accept authority or not. The essence of the power concept, i.e., the overcoming of resistance, explicitly includes cases for which the conditions for submission may be completely determined by the party having the greatest resources. Or, somewhat simplified, the power concept directs our attention to the dominating part in a relationship, whereas the concept of authority emphasizes the importance of the subordinate's acceptance (cf. Krupp, 1961, pp. 101-105).

As an example of the interpretation of the concept of authority, let me cite Swedish business economist Ramström. In connection with Simon's definition, Ramström (1964) says that it is clear that

> authority, in contrast to what is usually assumed, is "delegated" from below upwards. Instead of assuming that authority is distributed hierarchically downwards by the management, we may say that it is the subordinates who provide authority for the superordinate by accepting his directives. (p. 35)

According to Ramström, the rights of the dominating part to exert influence becomes a kind of present from the subordinates. This may be seen as a reformulation of Simon's (1947/1957) recommendation not to overemphasize the "arbitrary" aspect of authority.

The choice one makes between these theoretical concepts depends on the general image of organizations that one considers to be the most important and fruitful. The concept of authority is intimately connected with the systems approach to organizations and, therefore with the claims made by the proponents of this theory. The representatives of systems thinking recommend themselves, as we have seen, sometimes by emphasizing their "scientific" approach. However, systems theory also lends itself fairly easily to purposes whose value to its user may be more ideological than scientific.

The Inducement-Contribution Balance

One of the cornerstones of the systems perspective in organizational sociology is the notion taken from Barnard and Simon of the propensity of individuals to strive for a positive balance of rewards (surplus of *inducements* over *contributions*). This, in turn, is another formulation of the utilitarian doctrine of the individual's striving to maximize satisfaction and minimize pain. In the continuation of this section, I shall summarize some principal viewpoints that I developed in connection with a critique of Homans's exchange theory (Abrahamsson, 1970), viewpoints that are also relevant to the treatment of systems theory.

Homans emphasizes that the basis of all social science theory is psychological postulates. He states that these postulates are well known from learning theory and are often used either explicitly or implicitly in common parlance among laypersons. What are these postulates? The three most important ones are

> (1) If in the past the occurrence of a particular stimulus-situation has been the occasion on which a man's activity has been rewarded, then the more similar the present stimulus-situation is to the past one, the more likely he is to emit the activity, or some similar activity, now.
>
> (2) The more often within a given period of time a man's activity rewards the activity of another, the more often the other will emit the activity.
>
> (3) The more valuable to a man a unit of the activity another gives him, the more often he will emit activity rewarded by the activity of the other (Homans, 1961, pp. 53-55; cf. 1967, pp. 35-37).

Propositions 1 and 2 are variants of Thorndike's well-known "law of effect"; proposition 3 is primarily taken from elementary economic theory. Homans's (1961) most important point is that psychological and economic postulates are variations of one and the same general idea: "Both behavioral psychology and elementary economics envisage human behavior as a function of its pay-off: in amount and kind it depends on the amount and kind of reward and punishment it fetches" (p. 13).

A major problem with utilitarian-hedonistic theory, as it is employed by Homans and March and Simon is that the concepts of reward and punishment (pleasure and pain) are extremely difficult to operationalize. The predictions one can make on the basis of the theory are of the type in a certain situation the individual tries to maximize his profit, i.e., he will choose from a number of acts that act which is likely to give the largest reward and involve the lowest costs. This is, however, a rather vague prediction, because it remains to be specified which values the individual tries to maximize. Only when the statement has been specified with reference to these and only when these values can be measured is it possible to conclude whether the prediction was correct or not. Homans does not set any limits for what can be a value to a person. In fact anything can be a reward. It is rewarding to husband one's resources, but it may also be rewarding not to husband one's resources (Homans, 1961, pp. 79-80). It is rewarding to be an egoist, but also to be an altruist (p. 79). One achieves rewards by conforming, but also by not conforming (p. 118). There are potential rewards in the fact that the price of a commodity is low, but also in that it is high (p. 49). (For a longer discussion, see Abrahamsson, 1970, pp. 279-281. An extensive critique of exchange theory is given by Skidmore, 1975, pp. 114-122. It is remarkable that the hedonistic model is put forward by March and Simon, writers who otherwise are prone to emphasize the difficulty for the individual to predict and evaluate the results of his or her actions. If the person himself or herself experienced these difficulties, it would seem that it would be even harder for an outside observer.)

Thus the critique that may be leveled against the theses of inducement-contribution theory is not that it explains too little, but that it explains too much. In fact, there is no behavior of the organization's stakeholders that may *not* be interpreted in terms of inducements and contributions. According to the one, if a stakeholder chooses to remain in his or her relationship with the organization, this means that he or she perceives that the rewards received from the organization are greater than the contributions he or she gives to it. Analogously, if the individual chooses to withdraw his or her cooperation from the organization, this means the individual considers his or her contributions to exceed that which can be gotten from the organization. However, the theory is remarkably silent about what actually constitutes rewards and contributions (and, even more important, what is not a reward or a contribution) and how the balance between these two factors should be measured. It lends itself easily to ex post facto explanations but is weak on predictions.

Who Is a "Member"?

In the literature on systems theory, one often finds the term *member* as a label for single actors within the system. Katz and Kahn (1966) emphasize, for example, the risk inherent in the fact that an outside observer may equate "the purposes or goals of organizations with the purposes and goals of individual members" (p. 15). Ramström (1964) describes the organization in March and Simon's balance terms and adds: "The members of the organization are willing to remain with it only to the extent that their contributions do not exceed the advantages they get from participating" (p. 23). Caplow (1964) defines an organization as a social system with an unequivocal collective identity, an exact "roster of members," a program of activity, and "procedures for replacing members" (p. 1). Likert (1961) cites studies according to which high-productive managers differ from low-productive managers by generally having more positive attitudes to "every member of the organization" (p. 96). Simon (1947/1957) discusses "the means the organization employs to influence the decisions of individual members" (pp. 102-103) (i.e., division of work and establishment of standard practices).

This conceptualization of member is problematical in that, among other things, the formal aspects of membership are not clearly separated from the informal ones. The fact that the individual has a contract relationship to the enterprise, i.e., is an employee, tends to be associated with the assumption that he or she is also in general agreement with the organization's goals and values. *Member* implies that one actively takes part in, and gives support to, the organization in which he or she is working. However, formal employment (objective membership) should be distinguished from the degree of support and positive sentiments given to the organization (subjective membership).

The concept of member is used as a counterpart to thesis of balance between inducements and contributions and gives increased strength to the harmony model of systems theory. The problems that one meets in using the term *member* are well illustrated by the introduction to one of the classical contributions to organizational sociology, i.e., Blau and Scott's (1962) *Formal Organizations.* According to them organizations may be classified by reference to prime beneficiary (the cui bono criterion). By the use of this criterion, they distinguish between four broad classes of organizations:

1. Mutual benefit associations (in which the organizational members themselves are the prime beneficiaries).
2. Business concerns (owners as prime beneficiaries).
3. Service organizations (e.g., hospitals, schools, etc., with clients as prime beneficiaries).
4. Commonweal organizations (e.g., the police, fire protection, defense, etc., with the general public as prime beneficiary).

By using this interest group analysis, Blau and Scott's book separates itself from the mainstream of contributions to organizational theory. When they discuss the emergence of organizations and the role of organizational actors, however, they, as well as the writers mentioned above, run into the problem of distinguishing subjective from objective membership.

They state the purpose of their book in the following way:

> This book is about organizations—organizations of various kinds, with diverse aims, of varying size and complexity, and with different characteristics. What they all have in common is that a number of men have become organized into a social unit—an organization—that has been established for the explicit purpose of achieving certain goals. (Blau & Scott, 1962, p. 1)

But from where does the initiative to organize emanate? And whose goals are supposed to be implemented? The following quotation points to the answer:

If the accomplishment of a task requires that more than a mere handful of men work together, they cannot simply proceed by having each do whatever he thinks needs to be done; rather, they must first get themselves organized. They establish a club or a firm, they organize a union or a political party, or they set up a police force or a hospital and they formulate procedures that govern the relations among the members of the organization and the duties each is expected to perform. (Blau & Smith, 1962, p. 1)

The starting point is that some persons organize *themselves;* those who have taken the initiative to organize are treated as the members of the organization. The continuation of the authors' discussion, however, takes a different turn. At the end of the quotation, the initiators' role is to formulate rules of procedure that govern the duties of themselves and others who now have enlisted in the organization. The original initiators have assumed the character of superordinates or employers, and it is clear that *member* in the latter version also includes a position in the organization that is subordinate and dependent. The members of a police force are seldom identical to the initiators.

Thus there are reasons to be skeptical about the term *member* when it is employed by organizational writers. It often serves to conceal the fact that organizations are structures that have been deliberately constructed to meet the purposes of some major interest group or class (mandator), and that other members often have good reasons to be critical against these purposes (e.g., in the case when the mandator finds that the labor force is too large and decides that some should not continue as members, but must be fired).

Summary

The systems perspective is of dubious value as a basis for a theory of organizations. First, it avoids or ignores aspects of power. To the extent that dominance relationships are discussed, the proponents of this perspective strive to see these relationships as arrangements in which one party voluntarily submits to the other's authority. Permanent contradictions have no place in the systems perspective. Furthermore, writers in the systems tradition have obvious observation problems when the issue of organizational history arises. The reason for this is simple: If the hypothesis of balance of interests is accepted as a theoretical premise, there exists no need to describe and analyze the development of possible *forced* associations of actors to the organization and/or conflicts between different parties. The harmony assumption also seems to lie behind the employment of the concept of member, which frequently is used as a label for individual actors. The concept implies that those actors who are parts of an organization (i.e., who are objectively tied to it) also subjectively support the organization's goals. This is rarely the case with, for example, coercive organizations (the military, prisons, etc.). Even in organizations in which participation is in principle voluntary, there are usually large variations in the degree of subjective membership among the people working in the organization.

The fact that systems theory is based on assumptions of actors' needs for reward surplus (positive balance of exchange) and on other generally vague concepts makes it highly difficult to test empirically. Within organizational sociology and social psychology, the hedonistic-utilitarian exchange theory still has to prove its fruitfulness for further research.

I have also put forward some other points of critique, although they are of a more marginal character. First, system concepts lend themselves easily to descriptions of a reifying nature, such as using industrial production terms for public organizations, as was the case with hospitals. Second, the organic model, implicit in the systems perspective, may easily become biased in a manipulative direction, so that "disturbances" that have their base in conflicts of interest are explained to hamper the organization's achieving full health. Together these reasons are sufficient for a rejection of the systems perspective in organizational sociology. In the next chapter I shall try to sketch out an alternative model based on assumptions that are partly in opposition to systems theory.

Notes

1. A good summary of the major traits of the three traditions may be found in Scott (1967).

2. Among these should be mentioned some works by Gouldner (1954a, 1954b, 1959), Perrow (1967), and Woodward (1965).

3. *History* as an index word is absent from, e.g., Katz and Kahn (1966), March and Simon (1958), and Rhenman (1968, 1971).

9

A Process Model for the Study of Organizations

Introduction

Rationalistic theory and the systems perspective are in contradiction with each other on several points, the most fundamental of which concerns the notion of why organizations even exist. The answer proposed by systems theory is that organizations fulfill various necessary *functions*. Organizations represent the answers to different needs not only of the surrounding macrosystem but also of the different groups of stakeholders who, because of their relations to the organization, try to achieve a surplus of *inducements* over *contributions* (or at least an even balance between them).

The organization, or *vitalistic system,* also has needs of its own. It strives to survive and to preserve the balance needed to guarantee adequate contributions from the participations. In this endeavor, the organization is dependent on its relations to the stakeholders. Organizational balance is disturbed to the extent that stakeholders abandon the organization in search of better alternatives. The organizational leadership (or the enterprise leadership, because the theory is most often applied to this kind of organization) acquires the role of an interest administrator or mediator.

The rationalistic perspective seeks the answer to the question of the organization's existence in its *tasks.* The organization is perceived as a goal-directed structure, established by some party for the explicit purpose of getting some kind of work done. The different parts of the organization are subordinated to this purpose. Thus balance and equilibrium become relatively irrelevant concepts. To the extent that the parts do not fulfill their tasks, they may be exchanged for others. In direct contrast to systems theory, this exchange of parts does not necessarily involve a disturbance of the organization as a whole.

The antihuman consequences of the goals of Taylorism, to build organizational structures in which the individuals become little more than a complement to machines, have served for a long time as an argument rejecting the rationalist approach. Such arguments were further developed by the human relations tradition. Neither the negative consequences of the application of scientific management principles nor the discoveries by the human relations researchers are, however, sufficient reasons for rejecting the rationalistic approach. The idea of the organization being established to carry out specific tasks for the benefit of some party need not exclude a recognition of the importance of the informal structural factors, nor a critical attitude against extreme division of labor and fractionalization of tasks. As I have tried to show (in Chapter 8, "Reification"), the systems perspective also may be employed as a *machine theory* of organizations and may have the same reifying and manipulative consequences as scientific management.

It is true that the rationalistic perspective has some important shortcomings. Factors that limit rationality and that are related to conditions in the organization's environment are not adequately represented (Chapter 7, "External Forces"). This perspective lacks an awareness of disturbances that may arise because of inner contradictions in the organization ("counterrationality"; see Chapter 7, "Organizations Do Not Reach Their Goals"). Furthermore, its methodological complement, the means-ends scheme, possesses several built-in limitations.

The discussion below is based on the notion that it is possible to compensate for these disadvantages while keeping the advantages of the rationalistic approach. It should be particularly emphasized that the notion of the organization as an instrument for the implementation of interests is coupled to the existence of *different* interests in society (e.g., those of employers and employees). Thus for each organization it may be asked "For *whom* are its decisions and action rational?"

The process model to be developed below may, I hope, serve as a starting point for the study of organizations and as a basis for an analysis that clears away certain shortcomings inherent in rationalistic thinking. The model is developed to avoid the harmony assumptions of systems theory, its static perspective on organizations, and its general and diffuse conceptual apparatus.

Elements of the Model

1. Organizations Have a History. Organizations are created by a certain group of mandators. They develop and grow under the influence of this mandator group and are affected by various forces in the environment and by various inner logic factors (see Part 1).

2. Organizations Are the Products of Collective Consciousness.[1] Organizations are the instruments for the interests of mandators, and they are rationally planned structures for the fulfillment of these interests. As Boulding (1953) has pointed out, organization is "an expression of solidarity within the organized group, and . . . an expression of a lack of solidarity with those outside the organization" (p. 10). The organization may strive toward integration, but integration of whom and for what purpose? It is important to recognize that the framework of an organization normally contains conflicting interests and opposing powers, the details of which are "shaped by the broader environmental forces in society" (Krupp, 1961, p. 169). Thus "an emphasis on the integrating aspects of organization is but one among many ways of viewing organization" (p. 169).

3. The Mandator Strives Toward Full Rationality (Optimization) but Is Forced by Different Circumstances to Work at a Lower Aspiration Level (Satisfaction). The mandator (or his or her representative in the organization, see element 4, below) cannot expect that plans that have been designed will be carried out wholly in accordance with the blueprint. The rationality is circumscribed partly by economic, technological, and political processes in the society (e.g., business cycles, development of machines and information systems, contradictions between conservative and progressive groups, state interference). It is also circumscribed partly due to the organized activities of other mandators (counterrationalities).

4. The Mandator Is Usually Not Able to Run the Organization Completely on His or Her Own.[2] Even though a certain number of persons might have been sufficient for manning the organization when it started, this possibility usually decreases over time due to the growth of the organization and to modifications of external conditions. It is therefore a natural step that the mandator appoints a representative to handle the day-to-day activities of the organization. This representative is called the organization's *executive*. Motives for creating an executive are the need for a rational management of the mandator's time and his or her economic resources (the *economic* motive); the need for special knowledge to master different administrative and technical problems (the motive of *competence*); the need for long-range planning (the *continuity* motive); and the need to be able, if necessary, quickly to deploy the organization's resources in support of the mandator's aims (the *mobilization* motive).

5. The Executive Is Usually Appointed for the Task of Administering the Organization. To manage the organization's production, human resources as well as material assets are necessary. Therefore, the mandator and/or the executive hire a number of persons to carry out tasks at different levels and in different positions (officials and workers in staff and line positions). It is a problem for empirical research to define the executive independently of the rest of the labor force; more about this in the following discussion.

6. *The Size and Composition of the Labor Force (in Regard to Positions, Offices, Education, Age, etc.) Vary.* This variance depends on factors in the environment (material and social forces, competition from other organizations) and on the goals sought by the mandator and his or her representative.

7. *The Same Factors Also Affect the Structure of the Organization.* That is, these factors have an effect to the degree to which the organization approaches the mechanistic or the organic type. The existence of a certain structure depends partly on the plans by the mandator regarding production, personnel policy, etc. and partly on environmental factors that are difficult or impossible for the organization to control (market relations, legislation, etc.).

Elements 1 to 7 are summarized in Figure 9.1, which also indicates those areas that I believe are the objects of the three primary types of organization theory, i.e., the *theory of bureaucracy, administration theory,* and *sociotechnical adjustment theory.*

The theory of bureaucracy deals with the relationship between the mandator and the executive (see part 1). Administration theory analyzes the problems of the executive in its management of the organization's production. The two major areas of administrative theory are design theory, the development of ideas concerning optimum structure (cf. Taylor, Gilbreth, and various modern writers on, e.g., staff/line problems and matrix organization), and theories of decision making (e.g., Cyert & March, 1963; Simon, 1947/1957). Sociotechnical adjustment theory deals with problems that arise in connection with efforts by the executive to engage the employees in the organization's production. This area covers a great number of different theories that investigate the conditions for adapting human beings to technology and vice versa. They concern, first, the psychological and sociopsychological preconditions for creating such adjustment. Second, they deal with the practical arrangements for improving the adjustment to work (self-managing work groups, job enlargement, job rotation, etc.). Well-known examples are Blauner (1964), McGregor (1960), Herzberg et al. (1959), Friedmann (1955), Argyris (1964), Emery and Trist (1969), and Gardell (1971, 1976).

In order not to unnecessarily complicate Figure 9.1, I have excluded those boxes and arrows that would illustrate the parallel processes for other interest groups. An important cause of the emergence of an organization is the

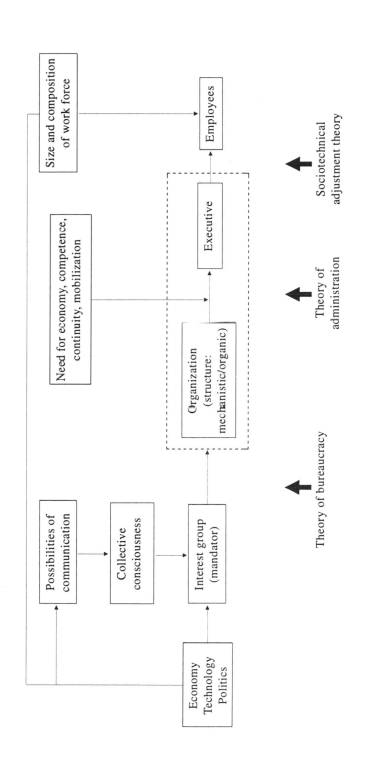

Figure 9.1. A Process Model for the Study of Organizations

existence of other organizations. The relations between employers and employees offer rich examples of this. Other organizations and their activities thus represent important conditions for the behavior of a particular mandator and his or her organization.

The Study of Organizations as an Interdisciplinary Task

Systems theory is typically presented as, and claims to be, a truly interdisciplinary theory, by encompassing elements from the biological, behavioral, and social sciences. While recognizing the interdisciplinary character of a theory as being of particular merit for the study of organizations, I believe that rationalistic models of the kind that has been outlined above offer at least as many advantages as systems theory. Consider, for example, the following research problem. Although hypothetical as presented here, it is a topic of great importance in the present economic and political situation in Sweden.

Traditionally, interest organizations have played a major role in the democratization of Swedish society. Cases in point are the role of the labor unions in the introduction of the 8-hour working day, old-age pensions, legislation for obligatory holidays, and solitary wage policy; the role of the workers' voluntary associations in the creation of a comprehensive system of basic and adult education; the influence of the abolitionist organizations on Swedish official policy on alcoholic beverages; and consumers' and housing cooperatives.

The growth of these organizations, and their gradually increasing fields of power and influence, also present some problems. As early as 1946, Heckscher (1946/1951), in his book *Staten och organisationerna* (*The State and the Organizations*) pointed out the tendencies to "free corporatism" that arose in the intersection between state and organizational power. Increasingly, the state had come to rely on the big organizations for achieving political consensus and obtaining the public consent needed to carry out various forms of legislation.

If anything, this role was further extended during the period after World War II. And as some writers have pointed out (see, for example, Elvander, 1976; Westerståhl & Persson, 1975), as various forms of interest representation develop, there is a danger that the fundamental principle of political democracy, "one man, one vote" will be eroded. To the extent that the organizations acquire direct influence in the political decision-making process, their members will gain an extra vote. This problem becomes particularly salient in public organizations (schools, hospitals, public-transport companies, etc.), which, according to the theory of parliamentary democracy, are to be governed only by the politically elected bodies.

If this is accepted as a legitimate problem for research, I believe that it can be fruitfully approached within the framework of a rationalistic, process-oriented model of organizations. Some examples of problems and questions for inquiry are presented below. I have chosen to structure the text with reference to three discipline areas (history, sociology/political science, and law) and to two aspects of organizational relations (internal and external). I hope that the distinctions between the six alternatives that result from this scheme will become clear as the discussion proceeds (see Table 9.1).

1. The emergence of labor organizations as expressions of group/class interests. The development of interorganizational linkages (for example, the association of individual trade unions) and patterns of corporatism (state-organization interdependence).

2. The historical development of mandator-executive relations (in each particular organization), for example, tendencies to oligarchy, bureaucracy and power crystallization. To what extent are certain functions and tasks concentrated in specific posts and individuals within the organization?

3. Conceptual/theoretical analysis of doctrines of (1) parliamentary-representative democracy and (2) organizational democracy (industrial democracy, economic democracy). What are the possible points of conflict and agreement? What contradictions, if any, exist between the public as mandator to the state and parliament and public employees as mandators to their trade unions)?

Empirical analysis of prevailing patterns of corporative relations: What influence can each particular organization exert on the state and the public representative organs? How do representatives of organizations look on their role as defenders of particular interests, in contrast to the safeguarding of the public interest?

4. Mandator/executive relations. What means do the members of the mandator group in a particular organization have at their disposal to control the executive? To what extent, and in what situations, are these means mobilized? How does the executive react in situations of internal/external cross-pressure (i.e., having to respond to demands from the mandator as well as from external forces, for example the state)?

Executive/employee relations: What means are used by the executive to control the employees and to secure compliance from them? What theories and doctrines are used to justify such control?

Mandator/employee relations: What latent and manifest conflicts, if any, exist between the mandator and the employees? To what extent, and on what grounds, do employees demand to be accepted as legitimate members of the mandator group? Does the mandator's definition of *organizational*

TABLE 9.1   Discipline Areas and Organizational Relations

Discipline	Relations	
	External	*Internal*
History	1	2
Sociology/political science	3	4
Law	5	6

democracy also include acceptance of employee representation in decision-making organs or is it limited to participation in direct production only (for example, through schemes of job rotation, job enlargements and other redesigns of the sociotechnical system)?

   5. *Description and analysis of legal rules* concerning political democracy and organizational democracy. Analysis of possible contradictions in the intersection of these areas. Analysis of rules for employee influence in public and private organizations: To what extent do they differ, and to what extent do they *have* to differ, if the principles of representative democracy are to be upheld?

   6. *Description and analysis of rules* governing—or supposed to govern—the behavior of the organization's executive (such as goal formulations, procedural rules, rules limiting the executive's right to independent decision making, rules resulting from the demands of external power central). How do these rules vary between different types of organizations?

Some Problems

   The application of Figure 9.1 in practical research leads to the following problems, among others.

   1. Definition of Mandator. I have identified the mandator of an organization in legal-juridical terms, i.e., as that person or group who has the formal right to appoint and dismiss the executive (see Chapter 1, "The Concepts of Mandator and Executive"). Two questions should be noted in connection with this. They concern, first, changes over time in regard to who is the mandator and second, the difference between formal rights and actual power.

   Changes Over Time. It is a quite commonplace occurrence that the original founder of an organization is not the same person or persons who currently form the mandator group. In turn, this means that the original goals may be far from identical to the present ones. Investigations of the composition of the mandator group at different periods of time may provide interesting insights into the conditions under which the executive works. Formal documents, protocols of board meetings, etc., are useful data for this purpose.

Formal Right Versus Actual Power. An essential question concerns the mandator's actual possibilities for controlling not only the organization, but more specifically, the work of the executive. Quite often, the mandator's influence is primarily exerted in extraordinary situations. That is, he or she is usually content to follow the activities of the executive in a very general way, limiting his or her own role to interference "in the last instance," e.g., to deseat or replace the executive. This is largely the case of the relationship between shareholders and the management in privately owned capitalist enterprises.[3]

2. Operationalization of the Model. One of the problems here concerns the study of organizational effectiveness. To some extent, the activities of organizations are determined by the goals formulated by the mandator and by the means that organizations employ in implementing them. To investigate the extent to which the goals actually become implemented, it is necessary (as I indicated in Chapter 7, "Problems of Method") that the goals be specific enough to allow determination of the degree of goal fulfillment. General and superordinate goals are of little use for this purpose, whereas goals at lower levels may be more easily operationalized. Furthermore, it is essential to investigate that definitions of effectiveness and efficiency exist within different groups in the organization, e.g., the executive, the mandator, and the employees.

Another problem concerns the delimitation of the executive. Like other employees, members of the executive (e.g., managers of private enterprises, high-level officials in voluntary organizations and in public bureaus) receive a salary from the organization for their work. How can one define the executive independent of the rest of the organization's labor force? One possibility is to begin with the fact that the executive group, being the representatives of the mandator, has a closer and more intimate connection with the mandator than other groups of employees. If this is the case, a sociometric criterion can be employed. Another possibility, that does not exclude the one just mentioned, is to base the definition on data concerning salaries and other benefits. Usually, individuals in executive positions have considerably higher salaries, more benefits, etc., than other employees. A third possibility is to examine formal documents, such as board minutes kept by the mandator. As a rule, decisions about the hiring and firing of members of the executive are formally recorded.

One may object to the first two approaches on the basis that they contain a certain amount of arbitrariness. Sometimes even employees at the lower levels have close contacts with the mandator, and certain persons in high positions may not have any influence on the daily activities of the organization. The difficulty in defining what is the "management" of enterprises is, however, also a familiar problem within the systems-oriented approach (see, e.g., Rhenman, 1971, p. 50).

3. Official and Operative Goals. Critics of the rationalistic approach have argued, among other things, that organizations often abandon their initial goals, that the goals are too vague to serve as guidelines for empirical research, and that new goals often arise during the organizations's day-to-day activities that often coincide badly, if at all, with the original purposes, and presumably also with the presently existing superordinate goals (see Chapter 6, "The Systems Perspective and Organizational Goals").

The very process of abandoning initial goals is, in itself, an important object for study, and should not be seen as a reason for rejecting rationalistic approaches. If superordinate goals are too vague, there are usually more concrete goal indications at lower levels that may be utilized for studies of effectiveness. The emergence of new goals as a product and consequence of the organization's current work appears, however, to confront us with a considerable problem. If the executive gradually replaces all goals with new ones, our ability to determine the raison d'être of the organization is seriously impaired.

In answering this objection, I would like to refer to Perrow's (1969) distinction between official and operative goals. The official goals of an organization "are the general purposes of the organization as put forth in the charter, annual reports, public statements by key executives and other authoritative pronouncements." Operative goals, on the other hand, "designate the ends sought through the actual operating policies of the organization; they tell us what the organization actually is trying to do, regardless of what the official goals say are the aims" (Perrow, 1969, pp. 369-370).

The official goals should be regarded as the general framework for the work of the executive that has been established by the mandator; the operative goals should be viewed as the ad hoc solutions proposed by the executive to handle those problems that arise in daily operations. If these solutions differ too much from the official goals, it is probable that the mandator will intervene to correct the executive. What is "too much" cannot be established beforehand. Rather, this determination is dependent on the judgment by the mandator himself or herself of the fit between operative and official goals.

Notes

1. The collective consciousness depends partly on the conditions under which each category of individuals lives and exists and partly on the possibilities they have for establishing contacts with each other. These possibilities, in turn, are determined to a great extent by technological factors (e.g., the development of systems for communication).

2. In an article by Greiner (1974), "The Developmental Phases of the Organization," it is argued that the first critical decision concerning the development of a newly formed organization is "to find a strong administrator who is accepted by the founders." This is because the growing activities of the organization means that the founders "are charged with a responsibility for management that they do not want to have" (p. 176).

3. An example is the following news item from *Aftonbladet* (December 20, 1974). "The executive director of Volvo, Pchr G. Gyllenhammar, 40, will meet his most difficult test when he is to confront the shareholders of Sweden's biggest enterprise at the annual shareholders' meeting. Influential sharcholders will make him personally responsible for the drop of Volvo's business index. In 21 months, this favorite share of the Swedish people has decreased in value by 180 crowns." Gyllenhammar, however, weathered the storm and did not have to take the post as county governor in Gothenburg, which *Aftonbladet* had assumed to be a definite possibility.

10

The Struggle Against Bureaucracy

To a very great degree, social life is organized life. The reasons to organize are obvious. Organization is a resource, a resource that can be used to reach common goals quicker and to combat opponents who have competing goals. Very often, organization is the most important resource that a group may command. It is a resource that can be sufficient in compensating for the superiority—materially and economically—of a competitor.

Bad organization can often mean defeat. This is a truism. More interesting, however, is the fact that *good* organization can also lead to defeat, i.e., for the purposes, goals, and interests that were the original reasons that a group organized.

Every organized group needs administration: An executive that carries out the decisions of the group and that, in day-to-day activity, strives to implement organizational goals. The problem that has been the focus of this book concerns the ways and means to ensure that the executive remains the administrator of group interests, to guarantee the executive's subordination to the mandator, and to prevent it from becoming a self-indulgent apparatus going its own way and becoming a bureaucracy.

The preceding discussion (see part I and part II, chapter 9, and especially Figure 9.1) suggests that the struggle against bureaucracy has to take place on two levels simultaneously.

A. The dependence of organizations on *external forces* (economic, technological, and political) sets certain limits for the measures that can be taken against bureaucracy. Conversely, to the degree that organized groups of citizens can liberate themselves from the confinement of material and other factors, their ability to control and exert power over the executive is strengthened. The increase in economic productivity in organizations and in society at large creates the possibility of reducing working hours, and consequently of gaining greater freedom to organize for the improvement of working conditions. Economic development also provides the basis for the improvement of education and culture. In turn, these may become the foundation for a critique of the existing production relations, and for the rational and deliberate changing of these relations. Furthermore, economic development is a prerequisite for extending the resources of underprivileged groups, and for creating the economic equality that, in turn, contributes to the implementation of democratic rule.

Economic relationships that retard the development toward greater equality and a heightened quality of life, constitute the material bases of bureaucracy. Thus, the elimination of bureaucracy, in the long run, is intimately connected with the development of the productive forces.

B. But bureaucracy also exists and is preserved because of factors that are *immanent* in the organization. Requirements concerning economy, competence, continuity, and mobilization automatically give the executive group a strong position. In the short run, and within the framework set by material conditions, the outcome of the struggle against bureaucracy depends on whether the executive group may be prevented from usurping the power of its special positions. How is this to be done?

I wrote in my commentary of Michels's (1958) book *Political Parties* that Michels primarily emphasizes the *form* of decision making and ignores the *content* of the decisions involved. "It is quite possible that even a very small group in the leadership of the organization, because of good contacts with lower-level members, can reach decisions that are in good accordance with the goals and interests of the mandators/participants" (see chapter 2, p. 79). The only *guarantee* for this contact with the nonexecutive levels and the only *safeguard* for this connection between the mandators' goals and the administration's day-to-day decisions is a broad participation among all organization members in the governing of their own affairs.

I especially stress *guarantee* and *safeguard*. Elite responsiveness *can* exist even in a system where the participation of citizens in politics is limited to the election of representatives at certain intervals. But the less the citizens participate in politics, the more the "people" become dependent on the benevolence of the "elite" and its motivation to respond to popular will, and furthermore, people become dependent on having a well-functioning competition among the elites. A participative system decreases this dependency and provides the possibilities for continuous control of the executive.

The primary characteristics of such a system have been sketched out by Marx (1933) and Weber (1968, p. 289). The former, but not the latter, believed in the possibility of implementing these principles: a delegate system based on conditional mandates, immediate recall of delegates, information duty for delegates vis-à-vis their basic organizations, and rotation of mandates. It is true that the realization of such a system will meet great difficulties. Differences in education and interests among delegates would render some delegates more powerful than others. The requirement of continuity in organizational management constitutes a pressure not to make mandate periods too short. But the participative system, in spite of these difficulties, represents a fruitful alternative for organizational leadership.

11

Organizational Research
and Rationalistic Theory

In this book I have dealt with arguments for and against the rationalistic perspective in the analysis of organizations. Compared with systems theory, its far more popular rival, rationalism has been treated with skepticism in the literature. With a few exceptions—Burns and Stalker, Perrow, and Krupp—there has been more of rejection than an attempt to arrive at a genuine understanding of the rationalistic standpoint. It is still possible to find in textbooks categorical standpoints that state that "organizations are open systems which characterize and are characterized by their surroundings" (Bakka & Fivelsdal, 1988, pp. 70-71).

What are the reasons for the skeptical attitude to rationalism in publications on organizations?

Rationalistic theory has been perceived as being closely connected with rationalization, i.e., methods used in industry and administration to improve productivity. Typically, rationalization has been achieved by carrying out time studies of work tasks and fragmenting these tasks into smaller work units, which are then spread among a number of workers along an assembly line. Similar arrangements have occurred in office work, for example typing pools, which are departments that do all the typing work in an organization.

The control of rationalization programs and their results has been one of the main tasks of work supervisors and middle-level management. Senior management has been responsible for ensuring that the final composition of these subtasks makes up a well-balanced whole. Large industrial companies and insurance companies have had at their disposal a comprehensive apparatus for measuring work performance and for making regular evaluations to ensure that the right combination of work processes is in use, i.e., that the means used achieve the intended goal.

The Machine Model

Goals, means, the division of labor, hierarchy, and bureaucracies are phenomena that many people see as being almost natural companions and as the main components of rationalistic organizational theory. Scientific management, of which Taylor and Gilbreth are the main proponents, can hardly be considered to exist outside the rationalistic frame of reference.

But rationalistic theory encompasses more than the rationalization movement and scientific management and contains many more interesting aspects than its critics have been able—or willing—to point out. To give an example, Taylor and Weber are often herded into the same rationalistic pen in organizational theory, even by authors who normally have no difficulty in seeing the difference between an engineer and a social scientist. The division of labor, hierarchy, and bureaucracy are often perceived as being parts of the same phenomenon, allowing Weber to be lumped together with Taylor. This may be exemplified with an excerpt from Fischer and Sirianni (1984):

> Emphasizing a clear-cut division of labor, scientific management has stressed the study of functional specialization, unity of command, centralized decision making, top-down authority, and narrow span of control.
>
> In addition to Taylor, the study of the formal (rational) aspects of organization has also been greatly influenced by the theory of bureaucracy put forward by the German sociologist Max Weber. . . . Weber was not concerned with a theory of organizational management per se, though his emphasis clearly resembles the tenets of scientific management. . . . [There are several] basic similarities between Weber's theory of bureaucracy and Taylor's concepts of hierarchy and specialization. (p. 6)

Fischer and Sirianni list the aspects that Weber has named as the distinguishing characteristics of the "ideal type" of bureaucracy (see Chapter 2, "Max Weber: The Theory of Administrative Evolution").

Fischer and Sirianni's way of writing is typical of the type of critique of rationalism that sees it as a mechanistic and closed arrangement of components; something that is a priori seen as an inferior analysis model to systems theory. Holistic, open theories that describe the organization as a system with interdependent interacting parts have been put forward as a way of escaping from this machine model (see Fischer & Sirianni 1984, p. 7).

As mentioned in Chapter 8, whether or not systems theories are noticeably less mechanistic is open for discussion. Today's computers are still machines, even though they communicate with their surroundings and are equipped with a feedback and self-correcting capacity. Should the organization then be regarded as a computer?

The most important question can hardly be "Which mechanical model is most similar to the organizations of today?" but rather "How far can a particular model take us in our study of a company?" What I wish to put forward here is that rationalistic theory can hardly be refuted by referring to its alleged mechanistic properties.

Critical Theory and Literature on the Labor Process

Another kind of criticism of the rationalistic theory is based on its use for practical purposes. Rationalistic theory comes under suspicion because of its links with different public and private sector power groups that attempt to achieve ever-higher levels of production efficiency. In this perspective, rationalistic organization theory becomes an instrument for the control and exploitation of employees.

Braverman's (1974) *Labour and Monopoly Capital* is the best known of the considerable number of books on the theme of the labor process. Others include Burawoy (1979), Edwards (1979), and Clegg and Dunkerley (1980); in Sweden, Björkman and Lundquist (1981), Sandberg (1980), and Alvesson (1983/1987a).

These works have a common orientation toward dominance and class relationships in the company. Conditions at the work place are seen to be substantially a reproduction and typification of class relations in the community in general. This theoretical school also focuses on the detailed forms of dominance, i.e., the real nature of overseers' supervision of work.

A major issue in this branch of organization theory is whether modern industrial production and office work impoverishes (dequalifies) or up-grades work tasks. Research, dominated by Braverman's dequalification theory, has hardly provided evidence that computerization would have the uniformly negative effects on jobs that many feared (see, e.g., Kern & Schumann, 1985). (This applies, mark well, to people who are in work; the extent to which the automation of industrial work is the cause of the enormous amount of unemployment we see today—a total of some 30 million people in the OECD countries—is still an open question).

The literature on the labor process represents what may be the most conspicuous reorientation of organization theory in the 1970s and 1980s. Here, research on organizations makes a marked departure from the technical orientation that was formerly commonplace. Braverman and his successors do not attempt to find solutions to practical management problems but seek answers to questions concerning the nature of work in the late industrial society. The answers are quite often formulated in Marxist terms, and it may be said that the publications on the labor process also extend historical materialism's area of interest.

In Chapter 2, I referred to Braverman (1974) and said that one weakness of Marxist theory was its inability to analyze social structure and class relationships at the microlevel.

It is—or has served primarily as—a theory for the analysis of macrolevel structures and class relationships and has rarely entered the factory gates. *Capital* contains very concrete observations of the nature of industrial work in 19th-century England, but these observations have not provided much general inspiration to similar studies.

As Olsson (1988) noted in a critical discussion on company management ideology and organization theory, labor process literature takes a new direction in this respect. In Olsson's view Marx did make important contributions to organization theory. A number of the organizational phenomena that Marx described, such as the transition from cottage industry to factory and the division of labor in a pin factory (under the manufacture system), are history. These particular circumstances can hardly be used to modernize the Marxist view of organizations. On the other hand, according to Olsson (1988, p. 28) Marx's analysis of the work process and the formation of value retains its interest. These are also the aspects that are further developed in literature on the labor process, albeit in what is sometimes a rather orthodox and uncritical manner (Braverman, 1974, is a good example), but also unreservedly and with interesting new approaches (see, e.g., Abell, 1988; Alvesson, 1987b; Edwards, 1978). A current Swedish empirical study of considerable interest is Johansson's (1988) work on Stocka Sawmill.

In Sweden, Alvesson (1987b) and others have reacted against what he calls the technocratic aspect of the existing body of literature on companies, and in the spirit of Marcuse would like to see a less one-dimensional organizational theory. The dominant stakeholders in the business world—represented by "business leaders and other members of the technical-administrative elite as well as owners of large capitals (Alvesson, 1983/1987a, p. 248)—are supporters of technological rationality. In its turn this rationality requires "a highly developed ideology which is capable of covering the contradictions and the criticism caused by technological rationality" (p. 249).

Organization theory has largely been an ideological instrument in the service of technological rationality. This is also true of organization theory when it has appeared in a "softer" form in, for example, the field of human relations.

> The advocates of instrumental rationality require, and make various efforts to stimulate the production of, consensus around the dominance of this rationality. . . . [An] important theme in the ideologies which support the dominance of technological rationality is the development of concepts and conceptions which lend to it a humanistic dimension. Such a development suggests that efforts are compatible with humanism and that the latter is almost a prerequisite for the former. Modern human relations theory (Maslow . . . , McGregor, . . . Schein . . . etc.) and authors inspired by this (like Peters and Waterman . . .) have contributed to the development and extension of these lines of thought. This organization theory has had a greater impact on the level of conceptions and ideas than in the field of concrete practice. In the formation of a consensus, it can be used in two ways. To start with, the organization theory bestows legitimacy on the predominant rationality, at a societal-ideological level and in respect to conditions in working life. In the second place, it constitutes a link in the process of qualification in the course of which individuals are fitted for practice within technological rationality (business leaders, for instance, as well as administrators and technicians, at the intermediary management level and higher up). (Alvesson, 1983/1987a, pp. 250-251)

Organization theory that claims to be "critical" must, says Alvesson, reject both the existing dominance relationships and the ideal of efficiency they are based on.

A similar contribution was made by Fischer and Sirianni (1984). They separate critical organization theory from company-oriented mainstream theory. In their view, the main line of organization theory is represented by literature that has an obviously technological-rationalistic perspective. This critical theory is, on the other hand, directed at class conflicts and power-related issues: It emphasizes the importance of social and historical contexts in the study of organizations, and it is also often skeptical about traditionally positivistic methods (Fischer & Sirianni, 1984, p. 13, cf. Alvesson, 1983/1987a, pp. 204ff.).

Fischer and Sirianni do not present the veneration of rationalization as a problem in itself in traditional management literature; it is rather the fact that what is considered rational in companies' reactions is defined solely on the basis of the mandator's interests. The owners and managers of companies consider efforts to constantly increase productivity as rational, since they are a prerequisite for greater profits and capital growth.

Fischer and Sirianni say that the employees get the worst of things in this process. They are exploited and become worn out both physically and mentally and a broader-based concept of rationality is therefore needed:

[The] search for a critical theory of organizations can be understood as an attempt to offset this narrow efficiency-oriented conception of organizational rationality. Much of the critical perspective can be interpreted as a search for a broader conception of rationality. . . . Antecedent to the problem of efficient work, organizations must be conceptualized as tools for the pursuit of personal, group, or class interests. (Fischer & Sirianni, 1984, p. 11)

Fischer and Sirianni emphasize that the business of organizations is not only with production but also with the politics of their associated interests. The task of the administrative system, which is often governed by the mandator's interests, is not only to produce products but also to "set the conditions under which production is appropriated, controlled, and distributed—in political terms, to determine what is produced and who gets it" (Fischer & Sirianni, 1984, p. 12).

The ambition of critical organization theory is to find ways to organize people in a way that utilizes their innermost abilities and finest characteristics. As the quotes from Alvesson, and Fischer and Sirianni show, various aspects of the rationalistic paradigm are seen as undesirable, alien, and injurious. In the words of the title of a well-known article by Argyris (1967), there is a difference between being human and being organized (see also Burrel & Morgan's, 1979, pp. 311ff., argument for an *anti-organization theory* aimed at achieving a radical humanism). In the critical literature being organized is, by and large, equated with being subordinate to rationalistic requirements and structures such as efficiency, hierarchy and bureaucracy.

Outer Forces and Inner Logic

There is an important difference between Argyris on the one hand and authors in the field of critical organizational theory on the other. While Argyris is in search of a reform of working life within existing political frameworks, the critical authors—headed by Braverman—see the shortcomings as directly related to capitalism. According to this analysis, it would be possible to abolish the division of labor, the pursuit of efficiency, hierarchy, and bureaucracy only if there is a fundamental change in the present conditions for production, for example, by the wage earners taking over the direction and allocation of work themselves. The outer force that is represented by capitalism determines the organization of work, and work organization becomes a means for capital owners to gain additional value (see Alvesson, 1987b, esp. chap. 5; Clegg & Dunkerley, 1980, esp. chap. 9; Edwards, 1979, p. 17).

A different interpretation is set against the above, one that is based on the idea that the inner logic in the process by which the work of large numbers of people is coordinated makes the occurrence of certain organizational forms inevitable. Irrespective of the social system, the ownership structure and the control system, motives of efficiency are to be found in all organized work, as is a hierarchical structure of positions.

In this approach, the hierarchy is a way of solving coordination problems in the most economical way possible. Similarly, one may ask whether efficiency and productivity are not universal values that every organization must attempt to achieve. Organizations cannot maintain their legitimacy merely by offering support and solidarity, i.e., what Williamson (1975) calls "atmosphere" (pp. 41ff.). Most organizations must also be able to show some form of production result. If the organization cannot supply what it says it has intended to supply, its reputation and credibility will suffer; not only externally but internally, among its own work force. With this view, the pressure for efficiency does not originate primarily in external power groups but is a direct consequence of the organization process itself.

The distinction between external forces and internal logic is a very important one in organization theory. Concepts like *power* and *control* take on strongly divergent meanings, depending on which of these two command perspectives is adopted. If the hierarchy is largely a product of internal logic, there is reason to question interpretations of the power relationship between superior and subordinate. It is generally true that the concepts of power and efficiency are often at variance with each other in organization theory and that interpretations made with the assistance of the former concept may sometimes become dissipated in efficiency terms (a longer discussion of the concept of external forces and inner logic is found in Abrahamsson, 1993, chap. 9).

"The dominance of technological rationality over the operational process corresponds to the interests of the predominating social strata" stated Alvesson (1983/1987a, p. 248) in one of his concluding hypotheses in *Organization Theory and Technocratic Consciousness*. Can then an organization theory for "the people" be made better—softer, more human, less technically rational—than one for "the elite"?

As the discussion above indicates, the elite in the organizations have a wide choice of ways to exercise their power over the people. According to mainstream theory the "hard" division of labor and intrusive supervision, and the "soft" human relations methods to increase productivity, adapt to one another. Power may be exercised in a variety of forms, all of which have a single purpose—to increase production. Therefore the answer to the question in the last paragraph can hardly be found in the appearance or form of the organizational arrangements. An employee-controlled company may also choose between hard and soft production and supervision methods. The important difference between it and the privately owned company does not lie in the degree of "technological rationality" of the methods used, but rather in the fact that the employees in the employee-controlled company have a choice.

The important point here is that the pressure for efficiency and technological rationality can be lifted (or lightened) if the actors in the organization are in control of the means of production, and they may choose "atmosphere" rather than "measurement" (Williamson, 1975, pp. 37ff., 45) by, for example, allocating time for members' meetings, courses of study, and leisure activities. In this case technological rationality assumes a different function than if the choice of the form of organization is made from outside and the employees have no alternative but to accept the decision. The form of the control method must, therefore, not be confused with the question of how the control method is actually applied. Employee-controlled companies may also choose extensive division of labor and the rigorous measurement of work performance in response to, for example, a fiercely competitive situation. Here too, the choice of production method is an obvious expression of technical rationality, but it has a different function in the micropolitics of the employee-controlled company, because the people who make the choice are also entitled to the revenues generated by whichever production method is chosen.

Another illustration of the importance of distinguishing between form and function is to be found in the concept of bureaucracy. Weber's "bureaucracy" is to be considered in relation to other ways of organizing society, through democracy and market forces, for example.

Although the market was Weber's ideal, he was realistic enough to see that the possibility of making it a reality was becoming increasingly remote. Weber saw the expansion of administrative strata—not least in large-scale industries—that became more evident toward the end of the 1800s, to be a threat to individual freedom as represented by the market and liberalism. Weber would like to have seen a civil society based on cultural values and with a substantial amount of individual freedom of action. Bureaucracy challenged this ideal. The threat did not lie in the organizational form, in which clerks were subordinate—Weber (1968, pp. 289ff.) was well-aware that this is hardly avoidable when organizations expand—but in the function of bureaucracy as a force that would turn society into an "iron cage." There is a more detailed discussion of the concepts of form and function in Abrahamsson (1993, chap. 9).

It is strange that Weber's remarks about bureaucracy as an organizational form has had such great impact on the literature. Weber has—not least in American organization theory—been portrayed as a theoretician of effectiveness and an apostle of technical rationality. He does not fit easily into current management literature, yet this has often been his fate. It is still possible to find statements like the following in textbooks on organizational theory.

> Weber's theory of "the superiority of bureaucracy" has been a red rag to the organization researchers of our time, who have been deeply involved in the study of the unfavourable effects of bureaucracy. (Bakka & Fivelsdal, 1988, p. 70)

As I have shown, it is these very "unfavorable effects" of rationalization and bureaucracy that interest Weber. However, the negative influence of bureaucracy relates to other factors than its efficiency. To Weber, bureaucracy represents an anomaly, a deviation from the social order he wishes to see realized. It is not a purely descriptive term, but rather a term with a partly polemic meaning, at least when Weber uses it to characterize the society in which he himself lived (see e.g., Weber, 1968, pp. 1410ff.). The concept is, in other words, not neutral in value terms even to the researcher who more than most advocated value neutrality.

But it is this very value neutrality that generally emerges in the use of bureaucracy in American organizational sociology. Scott's (1981) book *Organizations: Rational, Natural and Open Systems* is one of today's more widely read textbooks on the subject. On the subject of the ambiguity of the concept of bureaucracy Scott (1981) writes:

> The term [bureaucracy] also carries with it a great deal of emotional freight. For many the terms *bureaucracy* and *bureaucrat* are epithets—accusations connoting rule-encumbered inefficiency and mindless overconformity. Indeed, such views are probably those most commonly held by individuals in this society. By contrast, the foremost student of bureaucracy, Max Weber, used the term to refer to that form of administrative organization which, in his view, was capable of attaining the highest level of efficiency! (p. 23)

But it is the negative effects of bureaucracy on important values in society that is Weber's main point, a point on which he virtually disregards the efficiency of bureaucracy. Weber himself comes close to using *bureaucracy* as a severely critical term (if not as pure invective). In other words, one can hardly invoke Weber when, as does Scott (1981), an attempt at a value-neutral definition of bureaucracy goes no further than "a specialized administrative staff" (p. 24). If one wishes to avoid subjectivity, the words *official* and *administrator* would be far better choices. As I remarked in Chapter 1, the terms *administration* and *bureaucracy* are not synonymous.

(I find it significant that Swedish officials in public administration and government offices sometimes use the term *bureaucrat* to describe themselves. They should do so with caution: the term is charged with more than a century of subjective meaning that is not easy to pass off as a joke.)

The consequences of regarding bureaucracy as function rather than form are clear. If bureaucracy is to be abolished, then architectonic modifications to the structure of the organization are not enough. The issue to be addressed is the control of the way the administration wields power, aimed at ensuring officials do not assume the decision-making functions that are the traditional prerogative of the mandator.

So far, this discussion has focused on the potentially oppressive function that different technological-rational arrangements may have. My conclusion is that if the organization is an instrument for the pursuit of interests, we should study the use the mandator makes of different organizational means rather than concentrating exclusively on the form and appearance of these means. Strictly goal-oriented and structured work by no means excludes job satisfaction, provided I have been given the opportunity to take part in decisions concerning the organization of work and I can have some influence on the distribution of the results of production.

Soft Organizational Forms and Power

If we approach this discussion from the opposite direction, it also becomes clear that a "soft" organizational form does not necessarily involve a lesser degree of exploitation. A skeptical attitude to centralized management forms and efforts to find methods that permit both central control and some degree of local unit autonomy are fashionable among the management philosophers of today. This kind of reorganization may be presented as a form of democratization—for does not decentralization bring decisions closer to the employees?—and a fairly simple modification to form could thereby also be given a functional content (where the function in question concerns the dissemination of power).

Advances in computers are a powerful driving force underlying many organizational changes of this kind. If they are to be profitable, large computer systems must have many individual users. But when a large number of subordinate units are given the latitude to make independent decisions, these decisions may conflict with central management policy in a number of ways. However, there are at least two counterstrategies here.

The first is to use a *technical* approach to prevent the subordinate units from overstepping the mark (see Edwards, 1978). Computer system codes, passwords, and other access restrictions may serve to both limit and channel their use and, by registering the users of the various programs, they allow subsequent checks to ensure that the system has the intended spread. A central system can request details from departments and divisions and be instructed to sound the alarm—both upward and downward in the organization—when departments fail to achieve their set goals.

A second option is to internalize the policy of the organization among the employees, i.e., disseminate the policy in the most effective way possible in the form of internal training courses, videos, brochures, and company-specific symbols.

Selznick (1957; see Chapter 6 this volume) dealt with these processes under the heading of institutionalization. Selznick may be seen as a forerunner of the branch of organization theory that is currently involved with company cultures and symbolism (Alvesson & Berg, 1988). Here we are far from technological rationality in its traditional forms. The details in the management of an organization are set to one side and efforts focus instead on creating a common normative basis for all employees. The organization's culture is used to "govern the field of attention of the members of the organization and [define] governing criteria for how one is expected to act as a member of the organization" (Bakka & Fivelsdal, 1988, p. 118). To give an example, this is how the process of change was described in SAS at the beginning of the 1980s:

> It was a question of establishing a fresh set of common value standards, known to and accepted by all, i.e., a new cultural basis suited to the current SAS business situation and the general conditions in its operating environment, and which ensured professional service for its passengers. Here the organization's culture becomes a management system and it is of fundamental importance that the individual employee is very familiar with the new values, and is incorporated into the new order. (Larsen quoted in Bakka & Fivelsdal, 1988, p. 130)

When the organization culture has proved effective as a method of control one may use the popular call of the time of "Tear down the pyramids!" (Carlzon, 1985, a literal translation of the book's title), cut back on more traditional, formal, and external management and supervision methods, and possibly do away with a stratum of middle management. Whether or not this actually demolishes any pyramids may be strongly questioned (see Abrahamsson, 1993, chap. 7): The mandator usually retains the unrestricted right to direct and allocate work. The immediate detailed control of work has, however, softened, and there is broader scope for individual decisions at the lower levels. This kind of change, even if it is modest in scope and may be revoked, improves the job satisfaction of large groups of employees. For natural reasons, however, company managements seldom speak openly about the real motives for these organizational changes, preferring to equate changes in form with real functional reforms.

Systems Theory and Intervention

To summarize the discussion thus far, it could be said that the rationalist theory has been criticized for what has been seen as its concrete expressions: efforts to improve efficiency, the goal-means orientation, the division of labor, hierarchy, and bureaucracy. This criticism of specific rationalistic organizational forms may be found both in the literature on human relations and management and also in books on the critical theory and the labor process.

It is interesting to note that some of the forms by which people can be influenced and, for intervention in organizations, that have their roots in systems-theoretical premises have not attracted the same vigorous criticism. I refer here to sociopsychological confrontation techniques, T-groups, role-playing sessions, and the wealth of techniques developed within the framework of so-called organizational development. There is a large repertoire of methods with the common purpose of giving employees (or, to use the euphemism, "members of the organization") an "organic kick," that is, make them aware of the whole, the system that they are part of (see Abrahamsson, 1978). The basic theory of organizational development is that a change in individuals and their relationships also leads to beneficial changes in the organization (Berg 1988, pp. 17ff.; Berg & Wallin, 1983, chap. 3).

The relationships between theoretical premises and practical forms for influence are fairly clear in the rationalist tradition. The means are related fairly directly to the organization's goals. The relationship between goals and means is often more vague in the different "systemic" varieties of organization theory. It is not easy for a participant in a group dynamic exercise or a course in relationship training to see the connection between the content of the exercises on the one hand and the goals of the organization and the objectives of the mandator on the other. The Selznick-inspired institutionalization theory is clearer on this point, because it states explicitly in this context what results the process of influence should have: the companies' values, cultures, and symbols are specified in detail. (An interesting specification of this kind was carried out on behalf of the Norwegian universities by Hernes, 1988, esp. chap. 4).

It is to be expected that this latter category of methods for exercising influence becomes increasingly common as production is automated, investments in large computer systems increase, and the work force moves from producing goods to producing services. For, as Alvesson (1983/1987a) points out,

> To devote resources to increasing sensitivity and interpersonnel competence among workers whose tasks, due to noise and other physical restriction, do not permit social interaction with the environment (except perhaps during breaks) does not seem to be specially motivated from the point of view of efficiency. (p. 117)

An increase in the service content of production and a higher proportion of outward-directed and custom-oriented work tasks will lead to greater importance being attached to the methods for value institutionalization. While attention formerly focused on the ability of organization theory to identify key functions and strategic points for improving efficiency in the organization, there is a growing demand today for basic theoretical guidelines on how the company as a whole can be stabilized, presented, and given legitimacy. An inward-directed cultural revolution and outward-directed service management was the main outline of the 1980s in the field of organizations and thus also characterizes the tasks that today's organization consultants are working on (Brulin, 1987).

Toward a Mandator Sociology

What should, against the background outlined here, the program of rational theory be? I have already rejected the concentration on specific organizational forms as being far too confined a task. The rational theory has, partly erroneously, been seen as focusing on form and oriented toward efficiency. Which forms different organizational arrangements take is less interesting than the functions these changes fill in the micropolitics that constitute organizational life.

An organization is an instrument for performing work. But because it consists of people, it is a complicated and often strife-filled instrument. The empirical issues that arise are related to the causes of these conflicts: To what extent do they address the external properties of the work organization and work methods and to what extent are they linked to the way the executive promotes through his or her actions the interests that are the ultimate reason for the organization's existence? Sometimes these interests are unequivocal: The mandator is unchallenged as the head of the organization and the production goals are few and easy to define. However, the profile of interests often becomes complicated, maybe when what were once outside groups lay claim to the mandator's rights. Some examples are hostile stock acquisitions, government demands for employee representation on company boards, legislation that changes the ownership profile (note the debate and legislation on Sweden's employee investment funds), changes in the composition of government administration boards, etc.

But the interest profile may also be diffuse or contradictory (or both) if an organization is expected to achieve mutually conflicting goals. As, for instance, Berg (1981; see also chapter 6, "Balance and Exchange") illustrates with examples from the compulsory school system, there is a clear conflict between the set of rules that lays down grade marks, the obligation to obey, and specific timetables, on the one hand, and the edicts of the national curriculum on cooperation, democratic upbringing, and a holistic view, on the other. The goal of cooperation is not easily reconciled with the detailed ranking of pupils that the grade-marking system implies: The goal of democracy requires some relaxation of the regulations on obedience, and strictly detailed timetables are barriers to a multisubject approach.

Irrespective of the causes of these conflicts—conflicts of interest between different mandator groups and/or between stated goals—the executive faces a situation of contradictory rationalities. One of the most important tasks of rationalistic theory is to explain how executive management chooses to interpret these rationalities; how executive management can, against this background, formulate the day-to-day goals for the work of the organization; and how the results are evaluated and presented to the mandator.

The overall controlling factors for the rationalistic approach fall under the two headings mentioned above: external forces and internal logic. This does not, to return to the former group of factors, go as far as to establish that organizations are open systems that are influenced by their surroundings. The decisive empirical question is, of course, how this influence occurs, what the most important elements in the surrounding environment are, and what methods may be used to chart these elements and their influence. When it comes to inner logic, there are factors that are related to the mandator's assumption of risk, uncertainty, transaction costs, etc. i.e., factors that are of necessity attendant on the organization process, but are not for that reason more "systemic" than that which the mandator and the executive can, by means of rational computations and planning, compensate for.

I do not intend to discuss these questions in any more detail here, but refer the reader to Abrahamsson (1993, part II). Finally, let me summarize this chapter—and the main point of this book—by pointing out the need for a research approach in which the concepts dealt with above can be applied.

Research on organizations largely lacks a mandator sociology, that is, the detailed charting of the dominant interest groups in the community and the organizational instruments they have at their disposal. The 20th century has seen a sharp increase in the number of organizations companies, government authorities, trade unions, and voluntary associations in most industrialized countries. A glance at the yellow pages of the telephone directory over a couple of decades gives some support to this idea (see also Buksti, 1982, who gives general information on the growth of organizations representing various interest groups in Denmark). It is interesting to note that social science research has told us far more about citizens as individuals (i.e., as physical people) than about the legal entities (organizations) within which they spend a good part of their lives. The number of organizations, the spread of mandators over these organizations, their interaction patterns, factors that affect the growth and decline of certain kinds of organization, and the relationships between government and organizations (e.g., promoting or preventing their establishment) are just a few examples of areas of potential investigation for which our knowledge is nonexistent or, at best, fragmentary.

Some progress has been made, for example, in research on how company boards function (see Lundgren, 1982) and on the ownership profile of Swedish companies (see SOU, 1988, p. 38). However, the mandator function is largely uncharted by research. If we add the fact that we also know very little about the interaction between owner and executive management—i.e., between the mandator and the executive—then it becomes evident that a number of scientific dissertations are in search of authors. If this book can make any contribution to this research, then it has served its purpose.

References

Abell, P. (1988). Review of Mats Alvesson's *Consensus, Control, and Critique. Organization Studies* (9).

Abrahamsson, B. (1970). Homans on exchange: Hedonism revived. *American Journal of Sociology* (September), 273-285.

Abrahamsson, B. (1972). *Military professionalization and political power.* Beverly Hills, CA: Sage Publications.

Abrahamsson, B. (1978). *Den organiska kicken* (Working paper). Stockholm: Arbetslivscentrum.

Abrahamsson, B. (1993). *Why organizations.* Newbury Park, CA: Sage.

Albrow, M. (1970). *Bureaucracy.* London: Pall Mall.

Alvesson, M. (1987a). *Organization theory and technocratic consciousness. Rationality, ideology, and quality of work.* Berlin: Walter de Gruyter. (Original work published 1983)

Alvesson, M. (1987b). *Consensus, control and critique.* Newcastle-upon-Tyne: Avebury.

Alvesson, M., & Berg, P.-O. (1988). *Företagskultur och organisations symbolism.* Lund: Studentlitteratur.

Argyris, C. (1964). *Integrating the individual and the organization.* New York: Wiley.

Argyris, C. (1967). Being human and being organized. In E. P. Hollander & R. G. Hunt (Eds.), *Current perspectives in social psychology.* New York: Oxford University Press.

Asplund, Å. (1973). *Sjukvårdsadministration.* Stockholm: Läromedelsförlagen.

Back, K. W. (1972). *Beyond words: The story of sensitivity training and the encounter movement.* New York: Russell Sage.

Bakka, J. F., & Fivelsdal, E. (1988). *Organisationsteori. Struktur, kultur, processer* (with L. Lindkvist). Stockholm: Liber.

Barnard, C. I. (1968). *The functions of the executive.* Cambridge, MA: Harvard University Press.

Barnes, L. B. (1960). *Organizational systems and engineering groups.* Cambridge, MA: Harvard University, Graduate School of Business.

Bennis, W. (1959). Leadership theory and administrative behavior. *Administrative Science Quarterly* (December).

Berg, G. (1981). *Skolan som organisation.* Uppsala: Almqvist & Wiksell.

Berg, G. (1988). *Organizational analysis. Conceptual instrument and classification scheme* (Uppsala Reports on Education, 26). Uppsala: Department of Education.

Berg, G., & Wallin, E. (1983). *Skolan i ett utvecklingsperspektiv.* Lund: Studentlitteratur.

Berntson, L. (1974). *Politiska partier och sociala klasser.* Lund: Cavefors.

Björkman, T., & Lundquist, K. (1981). *Från MAX till PIA-reformstrategier inom arbetsmiljöområdet.* Lund: Arkiv avhandlingsserie.

Blalock, H. M., Jr. (1967). *Toward a theory of minority group relations.* New York: Wiley.

Blau, P. M., & Scott, W. R. (1962). *Formal organizations.* San Francisco: Chandler.

Blauner, R. (1964). *Alienation and freedom.* Chicago: University of Chicago Press.

Blegen, H. M., & Nylehn, B. (1969). *Organisasjonsteori.* Trondheim: Tapir Forlag.

Boalt, G. (1954). *Arbetsgruppen.* Stockholm: Tiden.

Boalt, G., & Westerlund, G. (1953). *Arbetssociologi. Arbetsbetingelser och mätmetoder.* Stockholm: Tiden.

Boulding, K. (1953). *The organizational revolution.* New York: Harper.

Braverman, H. (1974). *Labour and monopoly capital.* New York: Monthly Review Press.

Brulin, G. (1987). *Konsulten—en kunskapsförmedlare?* Stockholm: Arbetslivscentrum.

Brunsson, N. (1985). *The irrational organization: Irrationality as a basis for organizational action and change.* Chichester: Wiley.

Buckley, W. (1967). *Sociology and modern systems theory.* Englewood Cliffs, NJ: Prentice-Hall.

Buksti, J. A. (1982). Samspil mellem organisationer og omgivelser—tilpasning eller kontrol? In B. Öhngren (Ed.), *Organisationerna och samhällsutvecklingen.* Stockholm: TCO.

Burawoy, M. (1979). *Manufacturing consent.* Chicago: University of Chicago Press.

Burns, T., & Stalker, G. M. (1961). *The management of innovation.* London: Tavistock.

Burrel, G. & Morgan, G. (1979). *Sociological paradigms and organizational analysis.* London: Heinemann.

Caplow, T. (1964). *Principles of organization.* New York: Harcourt Brace.

Carlzon, J. (1985). *Riv pyramiderna! (Moments of Truth)* Stockholm: Bonniers.

Carr-Saunders, A. M. (1966). Professionalization in historical perspective. In H. M. Vollmer & D. L. Mills (Eds.), *Professionalism.* Englewood Cliffs, NJ: Prentice-Hall.

Clegg, S., & Dunkerley, D. (1980). *Organization, class, and control.* London: Routledge & Kegan Paul.

Crozier, M. (1964). *The bureaucratic phenomenon.* London: Tavistock.

Cyert, R. M., & March, J. G. (1963). *A behavioral theory of the firm.* Englewood Cliffs, NJ: Prentice-Hall.

Dahlström, E. (1956). *Information på arbetsplatsen.* Stockholm: SNS.

Dahlström, E. (1969). *Fördjupad företagsdemokrati.* Stockholm: Prisma.

Dahlström, E. (1971). *Klasser och samhällen.* Stockholm: Prisma.

Denitch, B. (1974). Självstyre och arbetarråd. *Tiden* No. 3.

Deutscher, I. (1959). *The prophet unarmed: Trotsky 1921-1929.* London: Oxford University Press.

Djilas, M. (1957). *The new class.* New York: Praeger.

Edwards, R. C. (1978). The social relations of production at the point of production. *The Insurgent Sociologist,* 8(2-3).

Edwards, R. C. (1979). *Contested terrain.* London: Heinemann.

Eliasson, G. (1984). *Hur styrs storföretag?* Stockholm: Liber.

Elvander, N. (1976). Företagsdemokrati och politisk demokrati. In *Organisationerna i det moderna samhället.* Uppsala: Almquist & Wiksell.

Emery, F. E. (Ed.). (1969). *Systems thinking.* Harmondsworth, UK: Penguin.

Emery, F. E., & Trist, E. L. (1969). Socio-technical systems. In F. E. Emery (Ed.), *Systems thinking.* Harmondsworth, UK: Penguin.

Etzioni, A. (1964). *Modern organizations.* Englewood Cliffs: Prentice-Hall.

Etzioni, A. (1968). *The active society.* New York: Free Press.

Fischer, F., & Sirianni, C. (1984). *Critical studies in organization and bureaucracy*. Philadelphia: Temple University Press.

Friedmann, G. (1955). *Industrial society: The emergence of the human problems of automation*. New York: Free Press.

Gardell, B. (1971). *Produktionsteknik och arbetsglädje*. Solna: Seelig.

Gardell, B. (1976). *Arbetsinnehåll och livskvalitet*. Lund: Prisma.

Gardell, B., & Dahlström, E. (Eds.). (1966). *Teknisk förändring och arbetsanpassning*. Stockholm: Prisma.

Germain, E. (E. Mandel) (1969). *Om byråkratin*. Halmstad: Partisan.

Gilbreth, F., Jr., & Gilbreth Carey, E. (1972). *Cheaper by the dozen*. New York: Thomas Y. Crowell.

Gouldner, A. (1954a). *Wildcat strike*. Yellow Springs, Ohio: Antioch.

Gouldner, A. (1954b). *Patterns of industrial bureaucracy*. Glencoe, IL: Free Press.

Gouldner, A. (1959). Organizational analysis. In R. K. Merton, L. Broom, & L. S. Cottrel, Jr. (Eds.), *Sociology today*. New York: Basic Books.

Greiner, L. E. (1974). Organisationers utvecklingsfaser. In L. Rohlin (Ed.), *Organisationsutveckling*. Lund: Gleerups.

Gulick, L., & Urwick, L. (1937). *Papers on the science of administration*. New York: Institute of Public Administration.

Gunnarson, G. (1965). *Arbetarrörelsens genombrottsår i dokument*. Stockholm: Prisma.

Hall, A. D., & Hagen, R. E. (1956). Definition of system. In *General systems: The yearbook of the society for general systems research* (Vol. 1). Louisville, KY: Society for General Systems Research.

Heckscher, G. (1951). *Staten och organizationerna*. Stockholm: Kooperativa Förbundet. (Original work published 1946)

Hedberg, B., Sjöberg, S., & Targama. A. (1971). *Styrsystem och företagsdemokrati*. Gothenburg: BAS.

Heiskanen, L. (1967). Theoretical approaches and scientific strategies in administrative and operational research. *Commentationes Humanarum Litterarum 39* (2).

Hernes, G. (1988). *Vivat academica!* Oslo: Universitetsforlaget.

Herzberg, F., Mausner, B., & Snyderman, B. B. (1959). *The motivation to work*. New York: Wiley.

Homans, G. C. (1961). *Social behavior: Its elementary forms*. London: Routledge & Kegan Paul.

Homans, G. C. (1967). *The nature of social science*. New York: Harcourt Brace.

Horvat, B. (1969). *An essay on Yugoslav society*. New York: International Arts and Sciences Press.

Håkanson, K. (1973). *Socialism som självstyre*. Stockholm: Prisma.

Israel, J. (1971). *Alienation: Från Marx till modern sociologi*. Stockholm: Rabén och Sjögren.

Israel, J. (1972). *Om konsten att lyfta sig själv i håret och behålla barnet i badvattnet*. Stockholm: Rabén och Sjögren.

Johansson, A. (1988). *Arbetets delning: Stocka sågverk under omvandling 1856-1900*. Lund: Arkiv.

Karlsson, L. E. (1969). *Demokrati på arbetsplatsen*. Stockholm: Prisma.

Katz, D., & Kahn, R. L. (1966). *The social psychology of organizations*. New York: Wiley.

Kern, H., & Schumann, M. (1985). *Das Ende der Arbeitsteilung?* München: C. H. Beck.

Knox, T. M. (Ed.). (1942). *Hegel's philosophy of right*. Oxford, UK: Clarendon.

Krupp, S. (1961). *Pattern in organization analysis*. New York: Holt, Rinehart & Winston.

Kupferberg, F. (1974). Från Lenin till Breznjev. *Zenit* (1).

Langefors, B. (1970). *System för företagsstyrning*. Lund: Studentlitteratur.

Laski, H. (1930). Bureaucracy. In *Encyclopaedia of the social sciences*. New York: Macmillan.

Lenin, V. I. (n.d.-a). The state and revolution. In *Selected Works* (Vol. VII). New York: International Publishers.

Lenin, V. I. (n.d.-b). On the party programme. Report delivered at the Eighth Congress of the Russian Communist Party (Bolsheviks), March 19, 1919. In *Selected works* (Vol. VIII, pp. 335-356). New York: International Publishers.

Likert, R. (1961). *New patterns of management*. New York: McGraw-Hill.

Lindskoug, K. (1974). *Rationaliseringens institutionella-strukturella aspekt*. Unpublished manuscript. Department of Sociology, Gothenburg.

Lindskoug, K. (1979). *Hänförelse och förnuft. Om karisma och rationalitet i Max Webers sociologi*. Lund: Dialog.

Litterer, J. A. (1969). *Organizations* (2nd ed., Vols. I & II). New York: Wiley.

Lundgren, A. (1982). *Företagsstyrelsen—om ledamotskarakteristika i börsbolagsstyrelser.* Stockholm: EFI/Handelshögskolan.

Lundquist, A. (1957). *Anpassning i arbetet*. Stockholm. PA-rådet.

Lysgaard, S. (1961). *Arbeiderkollektivet*. Oslo: Universitetsforlaget.

Mabon, H. (1973). *Organisationslärans utveckling*. Stockholm: M & B.

Mandel, E. (1971). *Arbetarkontroll, arbetarråd, arbetarstyre*. Halmstad: Partisan.

March, J. G., & Simon, H. A. (1958). *Organizations*. New York: Wiley.

Markovic, M. (1972). *Att utveckla socialismen*. Stockholm: Prisma.

Marx, K. (1933). *The civil war in France*. London: Lawrence.

Marx, K. (1976). *Capital* (Vol. 1). Harmondsworth, UK: Penguin.

Mayo, E. (1933). *The human problems of an industrial civilization*. Cambridge, MA: Harvard University Press.

McClosky, H. (1958). Conservatism and personality. *American Political Science Review, 52,* 27-45.

McGregor, D. (1960). *The human side of enterprise*. New York: McGraw-Hill.

Meidner, R., & Hedborg, A. (1974). Den offentliga sektorns problematik. *Tiden* (2).

Merton, R. K. (1957). Bureaucratic structure and personality. In R. K. Merton (Ed.), *Social theory and social structure*. Glencoe, IL: Free Press.

Michels, R. (1958). *Political parties*. Glencoe, IL: Free Press.

Mouzelis, N. P. (1967). *Organisation and bureaucracy*. London: Routledge & Kegan Paul.

Nilstun, T. (1980). *Metoder för utvärdering av reformer i arbetslivet*. Lund: Department of Philosophy.

Norrbom, C. (1971). *Systemteori: En introduktion*. Stockholm: M & B.

Olsson, S.-E. (1988). Organisationslära, ledarskap och hierarki. *Bokbox* (95).

Parson, T. (1951). *The social system*. Glencoe, IL: Free Press.

Parsons, T. (1960). *Structure and process in modern society*. Glencoe, IL: Free Press.

Pelczynski, Z. A. (1964). An introductory essay. In T. M. Knox (Ed.), *Hegel's political writings*. Oxford, UK Clarendon.

Perrow, C. (1967). A framework for the comparative analysis of organizations. *American Sociological Review* (April).

Poulantzas, N. (1975). *Political power and social classes*. London: NLB.

Presthus, R. (1962). *The organizational society*. New York: Knopf.

Ramström, D. (1964). *Administrativa processer.* Bonniers.

Rhenman, E. (1967). *Företaget som ett styrt system*. Stockholm: Norstedts.

Rhenman, E. (1968). *Industrial democracy and industrial management*. London: Tavistock.

Rhenman, E.(1969). *Centrallasarettet. Systemanalys av ett svenskt sjukhus*. Kristianstad: Studentlitteratur.

Rhenman, E. (1970). *God och dålig företagsledning*. Stockholm: Prisma.
Rhenman, E. (1971). *Företaget och dess omvärld*. Stockholm: Bonniers.
Rizzi, B. (1939/1985). *The bureaucratization of the world*. New York: Free Press.
Roethlisberger, F. J., & Dickson, W. J. (1947). *Management and the worker.* Cambridge, MA: Harvard University Press.
RRV. (1971). *Effectiveness auditing*. Stockholm.
Sandberg, Å. (1980). *Varken offer eller herre*. Stockholm: Liber.
Schulz, T. W. (1971). *Investment in human capital*. New York: Free Press.
Scott, W. G. (1967). Organization theory: An overview and an appraisal. In E. P. Hollander & R. G. Hunt (Eds.), *Current perspectives in social psychology* (3rd ed). New York: Oxford University Press.
Scott, W. R. (1981). *Organizations: Rational, natural, and open systems*. Englewood Cliffs, NJ: Prentice-Hall.
Segerstedt, T. T., & Lundquist, A. (1952). *Människan i industrisamhället. I: Arbetslivet*. Stockholm: SNS.
Selznick, P. (1957). *Leadership in administration*. New York: Harper & Row.
Silverman, D. (1970). *The theory of organisations*. London: Heinemann.
Simon, H. A. (1957). *Administrative behavior* (2nd ed). New York: Macmillan. (Original work published 1947)
Sjoberg, G. & Nett, R. (1968). *A methodology for social research*.
Sjöstrand, S.-E. (1987). *Organisationsteori*. Lund: Studentlitteratur.
Skidmore, W. (1975). *Theoretical thinking in sociology*. Cambridge, UK: Cambridge University Press.
SOU. (1966). *Års långtidsutredning*, 1, 1965. Stockholm.
SOU. (1974). *Socialvården: Mål och medel*, 39. Stockholm.
SOU. (1988). *Ägande och inflytande i svenskt näringsliv*, 38. Stockholm.
Stewart, R. (1976). *The reality of organizations*. London: Pan Books.
Stojanovic, S. (1970). *Socialismens framtid: En kritisk analys*. Stockholm: Aldus/Bonniers.
Sunesson, S. (1973). Om begreppet byråkrati. *Häften För Kritiska Studier* (4).
Sunesson, S. (1974). *Politik och organisation*. Kristianstad: Arkiv.
Therborn, G. et al. (1966). *En ny vänster*. Stockholm: Rabén och Sjögren.
Thompson, J. D. (1967). *Organizations in action*. New York: McGraw-Hill.
Thorsrud, E., & Emery, F. E. (1964). *Industrielt demokrati*. Oslo: Universitetsforlaget.
Tomasson, R. F. (1970). *Sweden: Prototype of modern society*. New York: Random House.
Trotsky, L. (1969). *Den förrådda revolutionen*. Halmstad: Partisan. (Original work published 1936)
Trotsky, L. (1972). *Den nya kursen*. Kristianstad: Partisan. (Original work published 1923)
Walker, C. R., & Guest, R. (1952). *The man on the assembly line*. Cambridge, MA: Harvard University Press.
Weber, M. (1956). *Wirtschaft und Gesellschaft*. Tübingen: JCB Mohr.
Weber, M. (1968). *Economy and society* (Vols. I-III). New York: Bedminster Press.
Westerståhl, J., & Persson, M. (1975). *Demokrati och intresserepresentation—en principdiskussion*. Stockholm: Liber.
Whyte, W. H., Jr. (1956). *The organization man*. New York: Doubleday.
Williamson, O. R. (1975). *Markets and hierarchies. Analysis and anti-trust implications*. New York: Free Press.
Woodward, J. (1965). *Industrial organization: Theory and practice*. London: Oxford University Press.

Subject Index

Administration theory, 68, 132
Administrative efficiency, 13
Administrative system, 13
Assembly line, 76
Atmosphere, 149f
Atmosphere vs. measurement, 150
Authority vs. power, 121ff
Autocracy, 5

Bureaucracy, xiv, 3ff, 48
   and capitalism, 39ff
   and power, 44f
   and the bourgeois state, 53ff
   as administrative system 9
   as rational organization, 5
   autonomy of in Marxist theory, 27ff
   autonomy of in Weberian theory, 42ff
   elimination of, according to Marxist the-
      ory, 31f
   elimination of, in Weberian theory, 35ff
   emergence of, according to Marxist the-
      ory, 23f
   emergence of, in Weberian theory, 35ff
   Marxist theory of, 21ff
   normative theory of, 20
   Trotsky on, 29ff
Bureaucracy theory, 132
Bureaucracy vs. administration, 151
Bureacratic ideal type, 37

Competence motive, 131
Conflicts in organizations, xvii
Continuity in organizational leadership, 49
Continuity motive, 131
Critical theory, 145

Debureacratization, 21
Decision, 82
Decision tree, 84
Democracy, 50

Effectiveness, 96
Effectiveness vs. efficiency, 107
Effectiveness vs. productivity, 108
Efficiency, 105, 111
Elite rule:
   autonomy of, 51
   elimination of, 51f
   emergence of, 48
Elites, 93
Energy as concept in systems theory, 111
Energy, psychological, 112
Equilibrium, 113f
Exchange theory, 89
Executive, 15, 131
   motives for, 131
Executive/employee relations, 135
Expertise in organizations, 49

About the Author

Bengt Abrahamsson is Professor of Sociology at the Swedish Center for Working Life (Arbetslivscentrum), Stockholm, and is also affiliated with Uppsala and Lund Universities. From 1980 to 1989 he served as editor of *Economic and Industrial Democracy,* and from 1972 to 1975 he edited *Acta Sociologica* (journal of the Scandinavian Sociological Assoication). Among his many publications are the books *Military Professionalism and Political Power* (1977); *The Rights of Labor,* with Anders Broström (1980); *Bureaucracy or Participation* (1977), an earlier English edition of *The Logic of Organizations*; and *Why Organizations?* (1993).